Mastering Podman

*A Comprehensive Guide to Container Management and
Deployment*

Robert Johnson

Published by HiTeX Press

For permissions and other inquiries, write to:
P.O. Box 3132, Framingham, MA 01701, USA

Contents

Introduction

In the evolving landscape of software development and deployment, containerization has emerged as an indispensable tool for developers and IT operations teams alike. Containers offer a solution to the perennial challenge of ensuring software runs consistently across various computing environments. As a technology built upon virtualization principles, containerization simplifies the process of deploying, managing, and scaling applications, encapsulating code and its dependencies into distinct operational units.

Podman represents a significant advancement in the realm of container management, distinguished by its architecture that does not necessitate a central daemon like its contemporaries. This feature grants users enhanced flexibility and security, as Podman supports rootless operation, thereby reducing security risks associated with privileged operations. Moreover, Podman's command-line interface mimics Docker's, enabling users familiar with Docker to transition smoothly to Podman with minimal disruption.

This book, 'Mastering Podman: A Comprehensive Guide to Container Management and Deployment,' is crafted to equip readers with the foundational knowledge and practical skills necessary to harness the full potential of Podman. From understanding the underlying concepts and architecture to configuring environments and deploying complex multi-container applications, this guide endeavors to cover all critical aspects of effective container management.

We begin by exploring containerization's history and significance before delving into the specifics of Podman as a container management tool. Subsequent chapters guide you through setting up your Podman environment, differentiating between containers, images, and registries, and mastering commands for container creation and management. As you progress, you will gain insights into networking, persistent storage, orchestrating applications with Podman Compose, and extending your understanding to advanced operations and security best practices.

Special emphasis is placed on security and performance optimization, crucial areas in which Podman's tools and features shine. This book seeks to impart readers with the ability to troubleshoot potential challenges and optimize container performance for their specific use cases.

By the end of this book, readers will be proficient in employing Podman to manage containers effectively in both development and production environments. It caters to both newcomers to container technology and experienced professionals seeking a deeper understanding of Podman's distinct advantages and features.

Our objective is to provide a comprehensive, insightful, and practical guide to container technology through the lens of Podman, supporting the reader in developing a robust understanding and mastery of this essential tool for modern software deployment.

Chapter 1

Introduction to Containerization and Podman

Containerization has evolved from its early origins to become a cornerstone of modern software deployment, offering isolation and efficiency. This chapter examines containerization principles and the benefits it brings. It introduces Podman, highlighting its architecture and differences from other tools like Docker. The chapter positions Podman within the broader container ecosystem, emphasizing its advantages and unique features, helping readers understand its role in efficient and secure container management. The comparative analysis with Docker and similar tools further grounds Podman's relevance and operational superiority in managing containers effectively.

1.1.   History and Evolution of Containers

The history of containerization technology reveals a fascinating journey of technological innovation, driven by the need for more efficient and isolated computing environments. At its core, containerization represents a pivotal shift from traditional virtualization toward a more versatile and agile approach to deploying applications.

The inception of container technology can be traced back to early isolation mechanisms in Unix-like operating systems. The chroot command, introduced in Unix Version 7 in 1979, was one of the earliest methods employed to alter the apparent root directory for a running process and its children. This capability allowed applications to run in a restricted directory tree, thereby providing a rudimentary form of isolation that laid the groundwork for future advancements in container technology.

```
sudo chroot /newroot /bin/bash
```

This command changes the root directory of the current shell to /newroot, effectively isolating the shell from the rest of the filesystem. Although chroot was a groundbreaking tool at the time, its limitations were apparent. It did not provide complete process isolation or secure separation between environments and was primarily a file system confinement tool.

As the demand for more robust isolation grew, technologies such as Unix System V Release 4 (SVR4) introduced jails in the BSD operating system. BSD Jails extended the principles of chroot by isolating both the file system and process spaces. The introduction of jails in 2000 marked a significant evolution in container technology, offering enhanced security and administrative controls.

```
jail /path/to/jail ip.address jail_name command
```

The innovation continued with the introduction of operating system-level virtualization within the Linux kernel, beginning with the Linux VServer project in 2001 and OpenVZ shortly thereafter. These technologies utilized the concept of separating the namespace of processes, allowing administrators to create isolated user-space instances within a single Linux kernel. OpenVZ, for example, provided containerization that supported multiple secure and isolated Linux containers within a single physical server.

Linux containers (LXC), introduced in 2008, capitalized on advances in Linux kernel functionality, particularly namespaces and cgroups, to provide the first true implementation of operating system-level virtual environments. LXC offered a comprehensive set of features to manage processes, network, and storage in an isolated manner without the overhead of traditional virtual machines. Unlike `chroot`, LXC was able to virtualize even the network subsystem, giving it a considerable advantage in terms of isolation and configuration capabilities.

```
lxc-create -n my-container -t debian
```

In parallel to these developments, the release of Solaris Containers in 2004 marked another significant contribution with the introduction of zones, which provided software partitioning to create virtualized operating system environments. Solaris zones offered virtualization at the operating system layer, establishing efficient management and high security between environments.

The most substantial advancement in containers came with the introduction of Docker in 2013. Leveraging LXC and later its own libcontainer library, Docker revolutionized the concept of containers by introducing a simple yet powerful API, which, along with an easy-to-use interface, significantly popularized container technology. Docker provided developers a tool to package applications and their dependencies into compact, portable containers that could run consistently across various environments, from development to production.

Docker's popularity ushered in a new era where container technology became mainstream, further catalyzed by its integration with DevOps processes. Its capabilities profoundly influenced concepts like Continuous Integration and Continuous Deployment (CI/CD), enabling seamless application delivery.

A contemporary innovation also worth noting is Kubernetes, an opensource container orchestration platform initiated by Google in 2014. While not a container technology per se, Kubernetes provides a platform for automating the deployment, scaling, and operation of application containers. It works hand in hand with container runtimes, abstracting away much of the underlying complexity and offering scalable, reliable operations that contribute significantly to the adoption and evolution of container technology.

Containers, since their inception, have evolved significantly from simple file system isolation tools to sophisticated infrastructure components crucial for modern application deployment. This evolution reflects an industry-wide movement towards distributed architectures and microservices, where containers serve as the foundational building blocks. Today, container technology underpins cloud-native development and microservices architectures, offering solutions that balance resource efficiency with strong isolation capabilities. Their ongoing development continues to explore the subtle interplay between speed, security, and versatility in software deployment strategies, as seen in recent explorations with lightweight container runtimes, serverless architectures, and edge computing paradigms.

The historical development of containers underscores an adaptive progression towards ever-greater efficiencies in computing. It reflects the pressing need for more agile, scalable solutions to today's complex computational challenges, aligning closely with advancements in cloud computing, DevOps, and distributed systems. Boundaries between containers and virtual machines continue to blur, and as container technologies further mature, their integration within hybrid and multi-cloud environments is likely to become even more pronounced, driving the next phase of innovations in technology infrastructure and application deployment.

1.2. Understanding Containerization

Containerization has emerged as a critical enabler for modern software development, deployment, and orchestration. By providing a means of encapsulating applications along with their dependencies, containerization has revolutionized the way developers build, deploy, and run software applications. Understanding containerization involves delving into its foundational principles and examining its benefits, implications, and practical uses in contemporary computing environments.

At the core, containerization can be conceptualized as an abstraction at the application layer that packages code and dependencies together. This packaging allows applications to run uniformly and consistently across different computing environments, such as on-premises systems, public clouds, or hybrid stacks. This relies on the host system's operating system to manage the application within its encapsulated environment.

Conceptually, containers contrast with virtual machines (VMs) in terms of the layers at which isolation occurs. While VMs virtualize the underlying hardware to run multiple operating system instances, containers share the same OS kernel of the host system and isolate applications at the user space level. This distinction results in several meaningful advantages for containers, including reduced overhead, greater efficiency, and improved scalability.

13

One of the most significant benefits of containerization is its contribution to consistent application environments across various stages of development and deployment. Developers often face discrepancies due to environment misconfigurations, commonly known as the "works on my machine" problem. Containers mitigate this by encapsulating application binaries, runtime environments, libraries, and configuration settings, ensuring consistency from development through testing to production environments.

The encapsulation model offered by containers supports efficient isolation. By leveraging technologies like Linux namespaces, containers encapsulate processes, file systems, network interfaces, and monitoring subsystems within isolated environments. This allows multiple containers to run concurrently on a single host without interference.

```
docker run --name=testcontainer -d nginx
```

Linux control groups (cgroups) further enhance containerization by offering resource allocation and limiting capabilities. Cgroups control the amount of CPU, memory, disk I/O, and network bandwidth available to container instances, ensuring that containers are adequately managed within the host's capacity.

Scalability is another pivotal attribute of containerization. Containers are inherently lightweight, enabling high-density deployment compared to traditional VMs. This lightweight nature allows for millisecond-level instantiation times, thus facilitating rapid scaling of applications. The agility to scale applications horizontally with containers is a cornerstone of modern microservices architectures.

Moreover, the portability of containers underscores their importance in today's DevOps-driven development culture. By abstracting application dependencies, containers allow developers to package applications into container images that can be consistently deployed across diverse environments, democratizing the application lifecycle management. The Docker image format, for example, is specifically optimized for delivering these portable application containers, supporting complex dependency management and version control.

```
docker build -t myapp:latest .
```

Containers play a crucial role in facilitating continuous integration and continuous deployment/delivery (CI/CD) pipelines. By embodying the deployment environment, container images are transportable across stages of a CI/CD pipeline without risk of environment-induced failures. This integration enhances agility, accelerates release cadences, and supports modern development practices focused on rapid iteration and feedback.

Beyond individual applications, containerization can be instrumental in orchestrating distributed systems and microservices. This orchestration requires scheduling, scaling, monitoring, and managing container lifecycles across distributed clusters—which Kubernetes excels at. Consequently, container orchestration engines such as Kubernetes are indispensable in managing large fleets of containers, providing capabilities including automated deployments, scaling, load balancing, and resilience.

Containerization's interaction with security paradigms is complex and multifaceted. While containers provide a degree of isolation by design, they also necessitate robust security measures, particularly when handling multitenancy in cloud environments. Container security considerations encompass image provenance, vulnerability scanning, runtime protection, and secure network policies. Tools like Clair and Trivy can be integrated into continuous deployment pipelines to automate security scanning of container images for vulnerabilities.

Despite these advances in security tools, the shared-kernel architecture of containers presents unique security challenges. Namespace utilization ensures logical isolation, but without proper configuration, privi-

15

lege escalation or escape risks persist. Applying systems like SELinux, AppArmor, and seccomp is critical to harden container environments against such risks.

Understanding the benefits of containerization also entails recognizing its inherent challenges and limitations. The learning curve associated with adopting container technologies and orchestrators can be steep, necessitating a cultural shift towards cloud-native practices within organizations. Operational complexity increases when managing numerous interdependent containers, leading to challenges in monitoring, logging, and troubleshooting distributed applications.

Furthermore, network configuration, storage persistence, and inter-container communication present nuanced challenges that require tailored solutions within containerized environments, achieved by leveraging overlay networks, persistent volumes, and service meshes.

Container technologies are evolving rapidly. Initiatives like the Cloud Native Computing Foundation (CNCF) and the Open Container Initiative (OCI) are foundational in guiding this evolution towards standardized container technology, ensuring interoperability and innovation. These open-source communities advocate for standards and best practices across container runtimes, orchestration, and associated tooling.

In essence, understanding containerization is recognizing its decisive role in aligning development capabilities with the dynamic demands of modern software delivery. Containers vividly embody the principles of microservices, automation, and scalability, enabling organizations to achieve goals of increased agility, enhanced efficiency, and reduced operational costs. They offer a flexible, efficient platform that bridges the gap between developer environments and deployment targets, empowering continuous innovation and comprehensive management of complex application ecosystems in contemporary infrastructure landscapes.

1.3. Introduction to Podman

Podman is an open-source container management tool that has gained significant traction as an alternative to Docker. Its architecture and features offer distinct advantages, particularly in terms of security, rootless execution, and compatibility with existing container technologies. Understanding Podman requires exploring its underlying architecture, unique capabilities, and its positioning within the landscape of containerization tools.

At its essence, Podman is designed to manage OCI (Open Container Initiative) containers and pods, with an emphasis on simplicity and adherence to standardized container specifications. Unlike Docker, Podman operates without a central daemon; instead, it manages containers as child processes spawned from the same parent process. This daemonless architecture offers several technical advantages, including enhanced security and user flexibility.

Podman runs without requiring elevated privileges due to its design. This capability stands out, particularly in contexts that emphasize security, as it allows the operation of containers in a rootless mode. By running containers with regular user permissions, Podman reduces the attack surface and minimizes potential vulnerabilities associated with running containers as root.

```
podman run --name=testcontainer -d nginx
```

Podman's rootless execution extends significant security benefits, especially for multi-user environments or development workflows, where granting root access might pose unnecessary risks. It leverages user namespaces, a Linux kernel feature that separates user and group IDs, to map a user's unprivileged UID to root privileges within the container, thus enabling container operations without elevated system privileges.

Moreover, Podman aligns with Kubernetes by supporting the notion

17

of pods, a group of one or more containers that share namespaces and storage, reminiscent of the pod concept in Kubernetes. This feature allows users to test, develop, and deploy similar container pod configurations both in isolated environments and in larger Kubernetes-managed clusters.

```
podman pod create --name mypod
podman run --pod=mypod -d nginx
```

Podman's ease of integration with Kubernetes is further bolstered by its k8s YAML generation capabilities. Users can generate Kubernetes-conformant manifests directly from running containers or pods, bridging the gap between local development environments and cloud-based orchestrated environments seamlessly. This makes Podman an attractive solution for developing containerized applications that are destined to run on Kubernetes.

Another pivotal feature of Podman is its Docker CLI compatibility. Podman's command-line interface mirrors that of Docker, allowing users familiar with Docker commands to effortlessly transition to Podman. This compatibility extends to supporting Docker Compose YAML files via the 'podman-compose' tool, facilitating the orchestration of multicontainer applications without significant tooling overhauls.

Among its unique offerings, Podman enables fine-grained image management via a host of features that offer more control over image storage and utilization. Through built-in capabilities, it manages container images with greater granularity, advocates for image security practices, and supports image signing and verification mechanisms like GPG signatures. This empowers users to ensure the provenance and integrity of container images being deployed.

Storage management in Podman is flexible, with versatile support for various volume and mount options. Podman can manage volume storage on the local filesystem as well as remote storage solutions, enhancing data persistence capabilities for containers operating in complex environments.

On the operational side, Podman offers lifecycle management for containers including creation, start, stop, restart, and removal capabilities akin to Docker. Automated workflows and orchestration are supported through Libpod, the library that underpins Podman, ensuring dependable container lifecycle operations.

```
podman restart testcontainer
```

As part of its security enhancements, Podman supports rootless networking configurations that align with CNI (Container Network Interface) standards. This integration facilitates the deployment of containers within diverse network topologies, providing connectivity and isolation based on user-defined policies.

Podman's integration with the broader DevOps ecosystem is robust, with tools for continuous integration and continuous deployment pipelines, allowing developers to incorporate container operations into their broader development workflows seamlessly. Its modular design and commitment to open standards make it an integrative tool in build pipelines, testing environments, and production deployments.

Podman's rising popularity can be attributed not only to its feature set but also to its transparency, being a key project under the umbrella of the Containers initiative by Red Hat. The community-driven development and adoption of open-source practices have fostered an ecosystem of contributions, plugins, and extensions that enrich its functionality and support diverse use, reinforcing its position in the container ecosystem.

Overall, Podman's architectural decisions, security orientation, Kubernetes alignment, and ease of use position it as a compelling container management solution. These attributes render it particularly suitable for secure container development, deployment, and orchestration in diverse environments, from local development machines to cloud-native platforms. In sum, Podman reflects a progressive evolution in container tooling, marrying the convenience of Docker-style operations with enhanced security and flexibility tailored to the needs of modern development and deployment scenarios.

1.4. Podman's Place in the Container Ecosystem

Podman's emergence as a prominent container management tool can be understood best by examining its strategic placement within the broader container ecosystem. The platform addresses specific gaps and needs unfulfilled by existing container runtimes and orchestrators, contributing to a diverse yet cohesive containerization landscape. Podman's unique contributions, its alignment with industry standards and trends, and its interoperability with other technologies underscore its significance in modern container ecosystems.

The Open Container Initiative (OCI) plays a central role in standardizing container formats and runtimes. Podman adheres closely to OCI specifications, ensuring that container images and runtimes remain consistent across different tools and platforms. Compliance with these industry standards enhances Podman's interoperability, facilitating its adoption alongside other OCI-compliant tools and fostering a broader acceptance within the ecosystem.

Particular attention should be given to Podman's daemonless architecture, which distinguishes it significantly from other container engines such as Docker, which relies on a long-running daemon to manage containers. By eliminating this component, Podman offers enhanced flexibility, as users can execute containers without requiring root privileges. This architectural choice aligns with the industry's growing emphasis on security and modular design, providing users with a more direct control model for container execution.

```
podman run -it --rm alpine sh
```

Podman's place is also solidified by its strong support for the Kubernetes ecosystem. The compatibility with Kubernetes, an undisputed leader in container orchestration, is crucial, as Podman allows users to create and manage pods using tools and commands that are consistent with Kubernetes principles. This capability not only facilitates the development and testing of Kubernetes-centric applications but also promotes seamless integration with Kubernetes environments.

Beyond Kubernetes, Podman is designed to work alongside other significant container orchestration frameworks and technologies. For instance, as a Red Hat (now IBM) initiative, Podman seamlessly integrates with OpenShift Container Platform, enhancing its capabilities within enterprise-grade deployment environments. Podman's design also complements the Red Hat ecosystem, providing a collection of tools that support comprehensive development, deployment, and operational paradigms across public, private, and hybrid cloud infrastructures.

Podman's roots in the Red Hat ecosystem position it as an ideal tool for enterprises seeking to leverage Red Hat's extensive suite of container solutions. OpenShift, built atop Kubernetes, utilizes Podman to manage local container workloads aptly, extending its influence across both development and production environments.

Moreover, Podman's compatibility with Docker commands fosters a bridge between the established Docker user base and new Podman users. By offering an analogous command-line interface, Podman lowers barriers for Docker users transitioning to Podman's safety-oriented, rootless model, fostering an expedited learning curve and easy adaptation.

Another important aspect of understanding Podman's niche in the container ecosystem is its focus on security features. Podman offers comprehensive security options designed to align with increasing concerns surrounding container security. Rootless operation serves as a foundational security measure, while other attributes, like SELinux integration, AppArmor support, and seccomp filtering, provide robust ways to ensure container isolation and protect against both internal and external threats.

Podman's capacity to work under rootless configurations is particularly valuable in multi-user environments. Such setups benefit from enhanced data security and stability by reducing the scope of potential container breakouts—where containers inadvertently gain unauthorized access to underlying host resources or other containers.

From a storage viewpoint, Podman's capabilities allow for integration with a variety of storage drivers and solutions. This versatility supports persistent storage solutions across dynamic, stateful containerized environments and offers a coherent approach to managing complex storage needs in conjunction with containers.

```
podman volume create myvolume
podman run -it --rm --mount source=myvolume,target=/data alpine
```

Network performance and configuration form another pillar of Podman's ecosystem relationships. Podman's compatibility with the Container Networking Interface (CNI) allows users to establish sophisticated networking topologies. These networking standards ensure that containerized applications handled through Podman have consistent, reliable, and secure network interactions.

Podman's position within the container ecosystem is also characterized by its contribution to community engagement and open innovation. As an open-source project part of the broader Containers initiative, Podman leverages community contributions to extend its functionality and maintain a rapid iteration cycle. This inclusion fosters an environment where new features, improvements, and integrations surface regularly, driven by collective input from developers, users, and enterprises.

As a testament to its ongoing evolution and ecosystem fit, Podman's toolset continues to expand, supporting containerized application operations across a diversity of infrastructural models, whether on laptops for local development work, in data centers for scaling workloads, or across distributed cloud architectures.

Podman's strategic fit in the container ecosystem underscores an evolving emphasis on lightweight, secure container management tools designed to align with open standards while offering robust integrations with various container orchestration systems. This exact role is instrumental for developers, systems architects, and organizations focused on harnessing efficient, secure tools to further their container and cloud-native goals. Podman's agility in such scenarios helps ensure that organizations can confidently leverage containerized operations tailored to their workflows and infrastructure environments, advancing the state of modern application delivery and operational model.

1.5. Comparing Podman, Docker, and Other Container Tools

The landscape of container management is diverse, featuring several tools that cater to different needs and preferences, among which Podman and Docker are most prominent. Each tool embodies unique characteristics and operational philosophies, offering a variety of functionalities suited to different use cases within the domain of containerized software environments. A comparative analysis of Podman, Docker, and other notable container tools illuminates their respective strengths, limitations, and ideal deployment contexts.

At the core, both Podman and Docker facilitate the creation, management, and deployment of containers based on the Open Container Initiative (OCI) specifications. This adherence ensures compatibility and operational consistency across container images and runtimes. However, differences arise in architecture, security models, and target user bases, leading to distinct operational paradigms.

Podman distinguishes itself through its daemonless architecture. Unlike Docker, which relies on a centralized daemon to manage containers, Podman operates as a command-line utility that directly interacts with the host's operating system. This design eliminates the need for a background service and enhances flexibility, particularly in multi-user or development environments where single-user operations suffice without modifying system-level permissions. Podman's native ability to execute in rootless mode offers a considerable advantage in terms of security.

```
podman run --name mycontainer -d alpine sh -c "while true; do sleep
    1; done"
```

Docker's architecture, featuring a long-running daemon, facilitates centralized management and orchestration of containers. This design supports complex container operations and streamlines multi-container applications' integration and deployment. Docker's daemon-centric approach is optimal for environments requiring extensive inter-container communication, e.g., orchestration and large-scale application deployment.

In terms of command-line interfaces, Docker and Podman exhibit similarities that make transitioning between the two relatively straightforward. Podman deliberately retains Docker's CLI syntax, allowing Docker users to adopt Podman commands with minimal friction. This compatibility fosters interoperability within developer workflows, enabling seamless transitions without significant rewrites of automation scripts.

24

A key differentiator is Docker Compose, a tool within the Docker ecosystem that simplifies the orchestration of multi-container applications by using YAML configuration files. Podman responds with `podman-compose`, a separate but analogous tool that reads Docker Compose YAML files, ensuring Podman's utility in managing complex container deployments similarly.

```
podman-compose up
```

Security remains a pivotal consideration in choosing between Podman and Docker. Podman's rootless execution model fortifies its security posture by minimizing the potential exploitation vectors available when containers run as root. Docker, historically running containers with root privileges, has introduced rootless modes in recent iterations. Despite these advancements, Podman's emphasis on rootless operations from inception provides a mature security model tested across various deployment scenarios.

Beyond Podman and Docker, container management tools like Kubernetes, CRI-O, and containerd play strategic roles. Kubernetes, though primarily an orchestrator, employs both Docker and Podman to manage individual container instances within large-scale deployments. Kubernetes abstracts away the choice of runtime to an extent, favoring container orchestration capabilities over specific engine features.

CRI-O, an Open Container Initiative-based container runtime, serves as a lightweight alternative designed explicitly with Kubernetes in mind. It optimizes Kubernetes deployments by interfacing directly with kubelet to manage container pods. Similarly, containerd—another Docker-initiated container runtime—operates beneath Docker's ecosystem and supports OCI standards, becoming increasingly typical as a direct substitute for Docker's own runtime in Kubernetes environments.

Another noteworthy tool is Buildah, which complements Podman by offering streamlined container image construction without requiring a full container runtime environment. Together with Skopeo, a tool for transferring and managing container images, this triad provides a comprehensive suite under the umbrella of Red Hat's container tools, suitable for diverse container manipulation tasks.

When evaluating choices among these container tools, several factors come into play, including usability, scale, security, integration capabilities, and ecosystem support. Each tool's characteristics align with different operational priorities:

- **Podman** excels in secure, lightweight, and development-focused environments with needs for tight integration and multi-container management without the necessity for centralized daemon processes.

- **Docker** remains an ideal choice for widespread adoption, robust community support, extensive ecosystem integrations, including interlinked tools like Docker Compose and Swarm for orchestration, making it an attractive choice for organizations with well-established Docker-based infrastructures.

- **Kubernetes** and its direct runtime associates (CRI-O, containerd) dominate large-scale and cloud-native deployments, effectively coordinating numerous distributed containers via sophisticated scheduling, load balancing, and self-healing capabilities to streamline intricate production systems.

Understanding each tool's respective ecosystem positioning enables developers, architects, and IT professionals to make informed decisions concerning containerized infrastructure design, aligning choice with organizational objectives, security requirements, and scalability goals. This insight empowers operative flexibility and ensures a robust deployment framework capable of sustaining modern application demands, driving agility, resilience, and forward-compatibility across diverse technological environments and strategies. As the container landscape evolves, these tools' standing and interrelations will continue to adapt, fostering new integrations and advancements within the containerization domain.

Chapter 2

Setting Up Your Environment for Podman

This chapter guides users through the necessary steps to prepare their systems for running Podman, detailing hardware and software requirements. It provides installation instructions for Linux, Windows, and macOS, ensuring a wide accessibility. Users learn how to verify successful installations and troubleshoot common issues. The chapter also covers configuring Podman for optimal performance and operation tailored to specific environments and use cases, establishing a crucial foundation for effective container management and deployment practices.

2.1.   System Requirements for Podman

Podman, a prominent container management tool, necessitates specific hardware and software configurations to ensure seamless operation across various platforms. Understanding these requirements is pivotal for users aiming to optimize their infrastructure for container workloads.

Hardware Requirements

The hardware prerequisites for Podman are influenced by the nature and size of workloads intended to be executed within the containerized environments. While the minimum hardware specifications can support small-scale deployments, medium to large-scale deployments necessitate more robust configurations. The following are the typical hardware requirements for operating Podman efficiently:

- **Processor:** A multi-core processor is essential, with a recommendation for at least a dual-core CPU for general use. For production environments, a quad-core processor or higher offers better performance.

- **Memory:** A minimum of 2 GB of RAM is required to run Podman smoothly, although at least 4 GB is recommended for running multiple containers or heavier workloads.

- **Storage:** At least 10 GB of free disk space is recommended for the installation of Podman and associated container images. With increasing container volume and more extensive images, consider provisioning with scalable storage solutions.

Software Requirements

Software environment compatibility is equally significant for Podman deployment. These prerequisites vary slightly across different operating systems:

Linux Podman is inherently designed to operate seamlessly across Linux distributions. Here's what you need:

- **Kernel Version:** Linux Kernel 3.10 or higher is mandatory as it provides the necessary functionality for containerization, such as namespaces and control groups (cgroups).

- **Package Management System:** Depending on your distribution (e.g., `apt` for Ubuntu/Debian, `dnf` or `yum` for Fedora/CentOS/RHEL), an up-to-date package management system is required to facilitate Podman installation and updates.

- **System Dependencies:** Essential utilities and libraries include `runc`, `conmon`, `slirp4netns`, and `fuse-overlayfs`. These dependencies handle container runtime and storage operations.

Windows Podman can be integrated into Windows environments using Linux distributions managed through the Windows Subsystem for Linux (WSL).

- **Windows Version:** Windows 10 (version 1809 and higher) is necessary to support WSL 2, which provides a full-fledged Linux kernel.

- **WSL Installation:** WSL must be enabled with a distribution of choice installed (commonly Ubuntu or Debian). Podman operates inside this subset Linux environment.

- **Virtualization:** Windows Hyper-V must be enabled to leverage kernel-based virtual machine capabilities.

macOS Podman functionalities on macOS rely on virtual machines to emulate a Linux environment.

31

- **macOS Version:** Big Sur (11.0) or later is recommended owing to improvements in virtualization technologies.

- **Homebrew:** An up-to-date Homebrew installation is useful for managing Podman dependencies on macOS.

- **Virtualization Software:** Software such as Vagrant or Docker Desktop supports creating and managing a Linux VM tailored for Podman use.

Implementing Podman across these varied platforms entails meeting the fundamental prerequisites prescribed above. However, fine-tuning the system resources available to Podman processes remains integral to achieving optimal performance.

For practical insight, consider the following illustrative command within the bash shell, exemplifying the verification of kernel version compatibility on a Linux system:

```
uname -r
```

The above command outputs the current kernel version, which is then validated against the requisite 3.10 or higher specification.

Verifying System Compatibility for Podman

Verification of system compatibility is not solely a matter of requirement checklists but involves proactive diagnostics to ensure each structural component is configured appropriately. This diagnostic cycle includes testing the interoperability of system components crucial to Podman operations and ensuring extended resources, such as storage and memory, function seamlessly under expected loads.

Consider using the following command to check available RAM in a Linux environment, a critical resource indicator:

```
free -h
```

The above command provides a human-readable summary of the memory status, aiding in aligning available resources with Podman's operational demands.

Furthermore, within the context of containerized environments, network connectivity is pivotal. Efficient DNS, gateway, and NAT configuration ensures containers maintain required connectivity for pulling images from registries and interfacing with external services.

Here is a basic example of a network diagnostic tool output:

```
PING google.com (142.250.190.174) 56(84) bytes of data.
64 bytes from mia09s28-in-f174.1e100.net (142.250.190.174): icmp_seq=1
ttl=115 time=9.65 ms
```

This diagnostic, using a simple `ping` command, verifies Internet connectivity—a quintessential factor for seamless container operations.

Podman User and Permission Requirements

The operational milieu for Podman extends beyond hardware and software, encompassing user roles and permissions. Non-root users can initiate containers, unlike other container management systems like Docker which often require elevated privileges. This function is facilitated via the `podman rootless` feature, promoting security practice by mitigating potential system-wide impact.

To utilize Podman in rootless mode effectively, the following configurations need highlighting:

- **User Namespace:** Enable user namespaces in the Linux kernel. This confines processes to their designated namespaces, improving security.
- **Subordinate UID/GID Mapping:** Employ `/etc/subuid` and `/etc/subgid` for mapping subordinate user and group IDs. An example entry may resemble:

33

```
alice:100000:65536
```

This entry indicates the range of UIDs and GIDs allocated for a user named "alice," facilitating identity mapping for containers.

In the evolving domain of container technologies, ensuring compliant yet efficient operating environments for Podman facilitates a robust and secure development and production lifecycle. By adhering to the outlined requirements and recommendations, users can capitalize on Podman's capabilities while maintaining system reliability and performance integrity.

2.2.   Installing Podman on Linux

Podman installation on Linux involves nuanced procedures that vary according to the specific distribution being employed. Catering to the package management system native to each distribution, users can facilitate this process through different installation methodologies— either utilizing pre-compiled binaries available via package managers or building directly from source, thereby providing flexibility and maintaining system integrity.

Overview of Installation Methods

There are two primary methods to install Podman on Linux distributions:

- **Package Manager Installation:** This method leverages existing package managers such as apt for Debian/Ubuntu, dnf/yum for Fedora/CentOS/RHEL, and zypper for openSUSE. The package manager method ensures ease of use, automatic dependency resolution, and streamlined updates.

- **Building from Source:** For users requiring specific versions or custom configurations, building Podman from source is recommended. This approach entails acquiring source code from the official repository, managing dependencies, and executing build commands.

Installing Podman via Package Managers

For most users, leveraging package managers simplifies the installation process. The following outlines distribution-specific installation steps for Podman using respective package management tools.

Ubuntu/Debian

For Ubuntu and Debian systems, apt, the Advanced Package Tool, facilitates installation.

```
sudo apt update
sudo apt install -y podman
```

This command sequence ensures repository metadata is current (apt update) followed by Podman itself. Users can verify installation and check the version with:

```
podman --version
```

If specific repositories are needed for newer Podman releases, integrate the Podman PPA (Personal Package Archive) as:

```
sudo add-apt-repository -y ppa:projectatomic/ppa
sudo apt update
sudo apt install -y podman
```

Fedora/CentOS/RHEL

These distributions utilize dnf or yum, depending on the version and policy. Here's an approach for Fedora and CentOS, with RHEL requiring subscription management prerequisite for any repository configuration.

35

```
sudo dnf -y install podman
```

CentOS users (version 8+) may require enabling the `PowerTools` repository or CentOS Stream before proceeding:

```
sudo dnf config-manager --set-enabled powertools
sudo dnf install -y podman
```

Verification is conducted through:

```
podman --version
```

openSUSE

For systems using openSUSE, zypper operates akin to other package managers, facilitating seamless Podman deployments.

```
sudo zypper install -y podman
```

This command ensures the Podman package is fetched and its dependencies resolved appropriately.

Upon installation, ensuring every necessary subsystem and service requisite to Podman's operation is functioning optimally remains critical. This involves examining network interfaces, storage drive capacities, and overlay file system configurations.

Building Podman from Source

For users seeking greater control over the Podman environment, building from source offers precision in terms of versioning and compilation flags. This flexibility allows optimization per specific hardware or software needs.

The standard approach to compiling from source includes:

- **Dependency Installation:** Essential development tools and libraries must be installed. On Fedora, these include:

```
sudo dnf install -y \
        gcc \
        gettext \
        glib2-devel \
        glibc-devel \
        device-mapper-devel \
        btrfs-progs-devel \
        gpgme-devel \
        libassuan-devel \
        libgpg-error-devel \
        go-md2man \
        git \
        runc
```

- **Fetching Source Code:** Utilize Git to acquire Podman's latest source code from its official repository.

```
git clone https://github.com/containers/podman.git
cd podman
```

- **Compilation and Installation:** Execute the build:

```
make
sudo make install
```

This process builds Podman according to predefined build configurations. Modifying the Makefile to tailor the build process can accommodate system specifications and performance mandates.

- **Verify Installation:** Ensure the compilation's success by inspecting the Podman binary:

```
podman --version
```

This command confirms the installed Podman version, affirming that the source compilation aligns with expected standards.

Users opting to build from source should develop a strategy for subsequent version management and upgrading procedures, ensuring that

37

future updates accommodate any custom-build specifications without disrupting operational stability.

Inspection and Diagnostics Post-Installation

Upon successful installation, validate Podman's functionality by performing basic operations. This verification phase includes executing a simple container run command:

```
podman run --rm hello-world
```

Upon execution, Podman fetches the `hello-world` container image from a remote registry, runs it, and displays a confirmation message for successful deployment:

```
Hello from Podman!
This message shows that your installation appears to be working correctly.
```

Should errors arise, re-examine configuration files, confirming network accessibility, and storage drivers compatibility, coupled with reviewing installation logs for potential anomaly or misconfiguration clues.

Engaging Podman on Linux through these methodologies equips users with a versatile and secure container management tool that integrates seamlessly within a pre-existing Linux ecosystem, allowing unbridled flexibility and performance efficacy.

2.3. Setting Up Podman on Windows

Setting up Podman on Windows is achievable through integration and interoperability mechanisms that enable Windows systems to operate Linux-based functionalities. Utilizing the Windows Subsystem for Linux (WSL), Podman can efficiently run within a Windows environment, leveraging a virtual Linux kernel to provide essential compatibility. This setup leverages the strengths of both Windows and Linux ecosystems, accessing the flexibility of container management on the reliability of Microsoft's desktop systems.

Preliminary Requirements

Before initiating Podman installation, ensure that the underlying system is configured to support WSL, a prerequisite for running Podman on Windows. Key preparatory steps include:

1. **Operating System Version:** Windows 10, version 1903 or higher, and suitable configurations in subsequent Windows 11 versions, are mandatory to support WSL 2.

2. **Virtualization Support:** BIOS-level options enabling virtualization, such as Intel VT-x or AMD-V, must be activated to facilitate WSL's virtual machine-based infrastructure.

Confirm the Windows version with:

```
winver
```

1. Verify virtualization support within the Task Manager under the "Performance" tab.

Installing Windows Subsystem for Linux (WSL)

WSL provides the necessary compatibility layer for Podman by hosting Linux distributions. The installation encompasses:

1. **WSL Activation:** Enable WSL and Virtual Machine Platform through Windows PowerShell with administrative privileges:

```
dism.exe /online /enable-feature /featurename:Microsoft-
Windows-Subsystem-Linux /all /norestart
dism.exe /online /enable-feature /featurename:
VirtualMachinePlatform /all /norestart
```

2. **WSL Update and Configuration:** Update WSL to the latest version and set WSL 2 as the default architecture:

```
wsl --set-default-version 2
```

Download the essential WSL kernel update via the Microsoft website to ensure an optimized WSL environment.

Choosing and Installing a Linux Distribution

Post-WSL setup, selecting and deploying a Linux distribution is the next critical step. Common choices include Ubuntu and Debian due to their wide community support. Install these from the Microsoft Store, allowing seamless integration into the Windows environment.

Verify the installation:

```
wsl -l -v
```

This command sets expectations by listing installed distributions and their version status, confirming WSL 2 is in operation.

Installing Podman within WSL

With a functional WSL environment, proceed to install Podman. Steps amount to installation procedures typically reserved for Linux distributions:

Ubuntu under WSL

1. **Update Software Repositories:** Ensure package lists are current to prevent installation anomalies.

```
sudo apt update
```

2. **Installing Podman:** Leverage the package manager for installation.

```
sudo apt install -y podman
```

This command installs Podman, adopting a consistent package source, thus securing dependencies automatically.

Verify Podman functionality resembling Linux environments by conducting a simple check:

```
podman --version
```

This command checks Podman integration inside WSL, confirming the installation's effectiveness.

Configuring Network Access and DNS in WSL

Network configurations play an essential role in ensuring connectivity for container operations, such as image retrieval and external service access.

1. **Resolve DNS Issues:** Modify the resolv.conf to maintain DNS resolution, allowing persistent adjustments accommodating network changes.

```
sudo rm /etc/resolv.conf
echo "nameserver 8.8.8.8" | sudo tee /etc/resolv.conf
```

This resolves DNS using alternative nameservers, enhancing stability.

2. **Check Network Adapter Status:** Utilize the `ip` command to verify network interfaces and ensure container connectivity remains intact.

```
ip addr
```

The command outputs network interfaces and verifies configuration integrity.

Handling Mount Points and File Systems

The interoperability between Windows and Linux environments manifests in managing file system mounts. WSL automatically mounts Windows file systems under /mnt, allowing windows-native and Linux operations to interact with the same datasets.

Usage and Operational Scenarios

Podman realized through this integration affords comprehensive container management use cases. Users benefit from:

- **Development Environment:** Utilize Podman for developing containerized applications within Visual Studio integrated directly through WSL.

- **Educational Engagements:** Leverage Podman to test container configurations and orchestrations, providing a sandbox to model deployments without affecting production.

- **Hybrid Workflows:** Coordinate Linux-specific scripts with native Windows utilities, combining the rich script library of PowerShell with Linux shell scripting through Podman.

Troubleshooting Common Issues

Encapsulated workflows ensure stable operation, yet challenges may arise, necessitating diagnostic procedures. Investigative processes for Podman on Windows emphasize:

1. **Verify Distribution Registration:** Check if WSL distributions are suitably registered.

   ```
   wsl --list --all
   ```

2. **WSL Backends:** Ensure hypervisor is perpetually aligned with version updates, maintaining full feature compatibility.

3. **Resource Allocation:** Configure memory and CPU allocations to prevent resource contention with other native applications.

Podman setup on Windows facilitates a profound capability expansion using WSL, blending the robustness of Windows interfaces with the powerful container capabilities endowed by Linux. By adhering to these meticulous procedures, users ensure a reliable container platform on Windows, capitalizing on dynamic toolkits, expansive application ecosystems, and multi-OS compatibility.

2.4. Configuring Podman on macOS

The configuration of Podman on macOS requires the creation of an intermediary Linux environment due to the distinct differences in macOS and Linux kernel architectures. macOS users can utilize virtualization technologies to deploy and run Podman, a practice that enables container management mirroring that of Linux systems. This setup leverages macOS's compatibility with development tools, which when combined with Podman's features, provides a robust environment for container-based workflows.

Preliminary Considerations

Several prerequisites must be satisfied prior to configuring Podman on macOS, tailored to utilize virtualization effectively:

1. **Operating System Version Compatibility:** macOS versions such as Big Sur (11.0) and beyond provide enhanced virtualization support, which is critical for running Linux-based features.

2. **Processor Requirements:** An Intel-based Mac or Apple Silicon Macs using Rosetta 2 for x86 applications are required. Ensure hardware virtualization features are enabled.

These prerequisites ensure sufficient computational resources for effectively running Podman containers within a virtualized Linux infrastructure.

Virtualization Environment Setup

Podman's deployment on macOS utilizes a virtual machine (VM) as an intermediary to run Linux container workloads. Various virtualization platforms can be employed to create this environment, with `Vagrant` and `Docker Desktop` being among the most prominent.

Using Vagrant

Vagrant streamlines virtual machine setup and offers seamless integration with various hypervisors. Proceed as follows:

1. **Installation of Vagrant and VirtualBox:** Install VirtualBox for VM management alongside Vagrant for VM setup automation.

   ```
   brew install --cask virtualbox
   brew install vagrant
   ```

2. **Vagrantfile Configuration:** Use Vagrant to define a VM that runs a compatible Linux distribution conducive to Podman. An example `Vagrantfile` could look like:

   ```
   Vagrant.configure("2") do |config|
     config.vm.box = "fedora/32-cloud-base"
     config.vm.provider "virtualbox" do |vb|
       vb.memory = "2048"
       vb.cpus = 2
     end
   end
   ```

3. **VM Startup and Access:** Initialize and launch the VM with Vagrant commands:

44

```
vagrant up
vagrant ssh
```

The above steps configure and access your VM environment through a basic SSH session.

Using Docker Desktop

Docker Desktop offers another pathway leveraging embedded virtualization capabilities and supports simple integrations for Podman.

1. **Install Docker Desktop for macOS:** This installation furnishes Docker's hypervisor infrastructure which Podman can leverage without separate installations of VirtualBox or QEMU.

```
brew install --cask docker
```

2. **Integration and Configuration:** Adjust Docker Desktop settings for optimal performance. Increase resource limits in terms of allocated CPU cores and RAM to meet Podman's workload requirements.

Installing Podman on macOS Virtual Machines

Once the VM infrastructure is in place, installing Podman parallels the common Linux installation process. Assuming the VM employs a Fedora-based distribution under Vagrant or Docker Desktop, use the package manager to set up Podman.

```
sudo dnf install -y podman
```

This step installs Podman and resolves dependencies, ensuring a functionally compatible environment for container orchestration within the VM.

Configuring Podman Operation

45

Podman's operational efficiency on macOS is configured by tuning resource allocation, storage settings, and network access control between the macOS host system and the Podman VM guest.

1. **Adjust CPU and Memory Allocations:** Using the Vagrant-file or Docker Desktop settings, ensure adequate memory (at least 2 GB) and processing power (minimum dual-core) are allocated to support container operations.

2. **Establish Shared Folders:** Configure shared directories to facilitate file exchanges between macOS and the running VM:

   ```
   config.vm.synced_folder "local_directory/", "/
   vm_shared_directory"
   ```

3. **Network Configuration and Port Forwarding:** Ensure containers maintain necessary external connectivity. Assign port forwarding within the Vagrantfile for accessing services running on containers:

   ```
   config.vm.network "forwarded_port", guest: 8080, host: 8080
   ```

Verification of Podman Setup

After completing the configuration, verify the effectiveness of the Podman setup using standard Podman commands, loading simple containers to check run capabilities.

```
podman run --rm -it alpine sh -c "echo 'Podman is running on macOS!'"
```

If successful, "Podman is running on macOS!" is printed, demonstrating successful execution and Podman's container capabilities within your VM environment.

Analysis of Use Cases

46

Podman's capabilities on macOS provide critical value, particularly across development, testing, and deployment scenarios:

- **Development Testing:** By simulating Linux environments in macOS, developers can build and test applications ensuring compatibility before deployment on Linux-based servers.

- **CI/CD Pipelines:** Integrate Podman within Continuous Integration environments to build, test, and manage containerized applications.

- **Educational Scenarios:** Boost learning environments for educators and students by sandboxing various Linux container applications within easy-to-use macOS desktops.

Maintenance and Upgrades

As Podman undergoes development, ensure periodic updates to both Podman and the Linux distributions in your VM to capture improvements in security, compatibility, and functionality.

Troubleshooting and Best Practices

Encountered issues range from connectivity problems to resource allocation conflicts. Here's an overview of corrective actions:

1. **Container Network Issues:** Investigate firewall configurations that may impede container network access, ensuring ports are open and correctly mapped.

2. **Performance Optimization:** Monitor resource usage ensuring the VM maintains ample resources, preventing slowdowns or crashes during high workload operations.

3. **Backup Critical Configurations:** Save important VM configuration files and container datasets externally to safeguard against unexpected system failures or reconfigurations.

By meticulously adhering to these configuration strategies, users can deploy a reliable, interoperable Podman environment on macOS, facilitating versatile container management workflows that meet diverse professional and educational needs.

2.5. Verifying Podman Installation

Verifying Podman installation is a crucial step that ensures the tool operates correctly across different environments, whether it's Linux, Windows utilizing WSL, or macOS with its virtualized setup. This process not only validates that Podman is installed but also checks the functionality of its core components, guaranteeing they are ready to manage containerized applications effectively.

Initial Verification Steps

First, confirm the successful installation of Podman by checking the version installed on your system. This can be ascertained using the following command:

```
podman --version
```

Typical output:

```
Podman version 4.0.0
```

Verifying Environment Variables and Path

Ensure that the environment path includes the directory containing the Podman executable. This is crucial for executing Podman commands seamlessly from any terminal session. Validate this by inspecting the PATH variable:

For Linux/macOS, use:

```
echo $PATH
```

48

For Windows, where PowerShell is in use, you can verify it with:

```
echo $env:Path
```

The output should include the directory path where Podman is installed, typically `/usr/bin/` for Linux, confirming that Podman can be invoked globally.

Functional Verification: Running Containers

To substantiate Podman installation, execute a basic container operation. This test checks Podman's ability to download an image, create a container, and run it, effectively verifying the core functionalities.

```
podman run --rm alpine echo "Podman is working!"
```

Expected output:

```
Podman is working!
```

This command downloads the lightweight `alpine` image, runs a trivial echo command within a container, and subsequently removes the container. Success indicates proper networking, storage, and environment configuration.

Networking and DNS Verification

Next, verify Podman's networking capabilities. Containers must resolve domain names and communicate over local and external networks. Test name resolution using:

```
podman run --rm alpine nslookup google.com
```

Expected output:

```
Server:      8.8.8.8
Address:     8.8.8.8#53

Non-authoritative answer:
```

49

```
Name:    google.com
Address: 142.250.190.78
```

This confirms that the container can resolve DNS queries correctly, an essential function for applications requiring Internet access.

Storage Drivers and Volumes

Verify the functionality of storage drivers and the ability to use volumes, which are critical for persistent data storage between container runs. Create a volume and use it in a container, checking data persistence.

```
podman volume create myvol
podman run --rm -v myvol:/data alpine sh -c "echo '
    DataPersistenceCheck' > /data/testfile"
podman run --rm -v myvol:/data alpine cat /data/testfile
```

The final command should output:

```
DataPersistenceCheck
```

This signifies data written in one container is accessible in another upon reattaching the volume, validating correct volume and storage driver operation.

Rootless Mode Testing

Podman's rootless mode enhances security by allowing users to run containers without administrative privileges. Verify this capability by executing container operations as a regular user:

```
podman run --rm alpine echo "Running rootless"
```

Expected output:

```
Running rootless
```

A successful execution demonstrates that Podman appropriately uses user namespaces to facilitate non-root operations, reducing potential

50

attack vectors common in traditional root-required container operations.

Common Troubleshooting

Inevitably, issues may arise during verification. Here are some typical problems and methods to resolve them:

- **Command Not Found:** Confirm Podman is in the system PATH or re-add it by modifying shell profile configurations (e.g., .bashrc, .zshrc).

- **Network/DNS Failures:** Inspect network settings, especially firewall or DNS server configurations, ensuring outgoing requests aren't blocked.

- **Storage Errors:** Verify underlying storage drivers. Podman's compatibility with various drivers (overlayfs, btrfs) ensures adaptability, but conflicts in configuration can cause failures.

- **Permissions Issues in Rootless Mode:** Examine user and group permissions; constraints in /etc/subuid and /etc/subgid mappings can restrict access to necessary user IDs for operations.

Example Scenarios for Practice and Proficiency

Beyond initial verification, pursuing practice scenarios expands users' understanding and proficiency in Podman's capabilities:

1. **Running Dual Containers with Networking:** Deploy two containers, ensuring they communicate over an encapsulated network created by Podman's default network driver:

```
podman network create mynetwork
podman run -d --name app1 --network=mynetwork alpine /bin/
sh -c "while true; do sleep 1000; done"
```

51

```
podman run --rm --network=mynetwork alpine ping -c 3 app1
```

Upon successful command execution, expect regular ICMP ping responses from app1, confirming inter-container networking.

2. **Building Custom Images:** Create a simple Dockerfile to construct a custom image, confirming Podman's image-building facilities.

   Create a Dockerfile:

   ```
   FROM alpine
   CMD ["echo", "Custom Image Running"]
   ```

   Build and run:

   ```
   podman build -t customimage .
   podman run --rm customimage
   ```

   Expect output:

   ```
   Custom Image Running
   ```

Verifying Podman installation and testing these frequently exercised scenarios guarantee an operational understanding of its container management efficiencies. Ensuring each component, from core functionality and networking to custom image creation, operates seamlessly underpins successful Podman deployments in diversified, production-grade environments.

2.6. Configuring Podman for Optimal Use

Successfully configuring Podman for optimal use involves customized adjustments and performance tuning to better manage containerized

workloads. Given that Podman operates without a centralized daemon, configurations should focus on enhancing efficiency, security,
and scalability according to specific workload requirements. This section delves into customizing Podman's storage, networking, and performance settings, facilitating peak operational capacity.

Storage Configuration

Appropriate storage configuration ensures container data processing
is both efficient and secure. Podman supports various storage drivers,
and using the best-suited driver can enhance performance significantly.

- **Storage Drivers:** Podman supports drivers such as `overlayfs`,
  `vfs`, and `btrfs`. The `overlayfs` driver is recommended for general use due to its high performance and low storage overhead.

  Configure the storage driver by editing the
  `/etc/containers/storage.conf` file:

  ```
  [storage]
  driver = "overlay"
  ```

  Confirm the current storage configuration:

  ```
  podman info --format "{{.Store.GraphDriverName}}"
  ```

  The above command should reflect the configured driver, ensuring alignment between intended use and storage strategy.

- **Storage Options:** Adjust storage options to fine-tune
  performance. Configure overlay sizes and limits in
  `/etc/containers/storage.conf` to optimize disk usage.

Networking Optimizations

53

Networking configurations in Podman should facilitate robust inter-container communications and external access. Configuring network settings optimally enhances container interaction and resource accessibility.

- **Custom Container Networks:** Construct user-defined networks to isolate and manage container traffic. This approach prevents network collisions and secures communication pathways.

```
podman network create mycustomnet
podman run --network=mycustomnet --name=myapp alpine
```

Use `podman network inspect mycustomnet` to verify network parameters and ascertain configurations.

- **DNS and IP Management:** Customize DNS settings in the `/etc/containers/containers.conf` for enhanced resolution control, ensuring all containers adhere to specified DNS servers.

Add DNS configurations:

```
[containers]
dns_servers = ["8.8.8.8", "8.8.4.4"]
```

Validate by running DNS-focused commands within containers:

```
podman run --rm alpine nslookup example.com
```

Confirm the resolution paths follow the appointed DNS servers.

Security Enhancements

Enhancing security optimizations in Podman helps mitigate risks, especially when managing sensitive data and public-facing services.

- **Rootless Containers:** Run containers in rootless mode for improved security infrastructure, minimizing the attack surface.

54

Example:

```
podman unshare podman run --rm alpine id
```

This command executes in a user namespace, verifying rootless operational status while protecting host system integrity.

- **SELinux and AppArmor:** Implement SELinux or AppArmor policies to isolate containers, ensuring each process adheres to predefined access controls.

  Check and enforce:

```
podman run --security-opt label=type:my_container_t myapp
```

Performance Tuning

Fine-tuning Podman environments includes adjusting resource allocations and container concurrency management, which is crucial for handling intense workloads.

- **Resource Allocation:** Define CPU shares, memory limits, and I/O thresholds to balance resource utilization.

  Command example:

```
podman run --cpus=2 --memory=512m --name=myapp myimage
```

This ensures the container uses a maximum of 2 CPU cores and 512MB of RAM, thereby preventing resource hogging.

- **Concurrency and Scalability:** Utilize Podman's pod concept to facilitate groups of containers with shared network namespaces, optimizing for scalability.

  Create a pod and add containers:

```
podman pod create --name=mypod
podman run --pod=mypod myimage1
podman run --pod=mypod myimage2
```

This organizes microservices under unified network configurations, simplified with shared resources, managed concurrently.

Monitoring and Maintenance

Robust management practices enhance operational stability and performance tracking within containerized ecosystems.

- **Logging and Metrics:** Enable extensive logging to capture and analyze container output and errors.

  Access logs:
  ```
  podman logs myapp
  ```

  Configure centralized logging solutions by integrating with system log services or third-party applications.

- **Regular Updates and Backups:** Perform routine updates to both Podman and related system components, securing latest features and patches.

  Comprehensive backup strategies encompass:
  ```
  podman save -o mybackup.tar myimage
  ```

  Regular backups should safeguard container images and volume data, facilitating recovery protocols amid failure or data loss scenarios.

Advanced Configuration Techniques

Explore deeper integrations, such as leveraging systemd for Podman services, automating container deployment with tailored service definitions.

- **Systemd Service Files:** Define and register Podman containers as systemd services to automate start/stop operations alongside system boot processes.

  Service example:

  ```
  [Unit]
  Description=My Podman container
  After=network.target

  [Service]
  ExecStart=/usr/bin/podman start -a myapp
  ExecStop=/usr/bin/podman stop -t 2 myapp
  Restart=always

  [Install]
  WantedBy=multi-user.target
  ```

  Enable and start the service:

  ```
  sudo systemctl enable myapp.service
  sudo systemctl start myapp.service
  ```

  This ensures container states persist through host reboots and automates management operations.

- **Cross-Platform Deployments:** Experiment with orchestrating services using Kubernetes or OpenShift to marry Podman configurations with larger-scale container orchestration platforms.

By diving into these diverse and nuanced configurations, practitioners ensure Podman operates with peak efficiency, securely and responsively, tailored to complex application landscapes and dynamic workload demands. This sets a foundation for both current use and expanding containerized strategies pivotal to modern computing environments.

Chapter 3

Understanding Containers, Images, and Registries

This chapter explores the core concepts of containers and container images, detailing their structure and purpose. It covers the processes for building images and the significance of layering for storage efficiency. Readers learn about container registries, with focus on their role in image distribution and management. Practical guidance includes pulling and pushing images and managing image tags and versions. The chapter concludes with a discussion on different image formats and compatibility, equipping readers with a comprehensive understanding of how containers, images, and registries interrelate within Podman.

3.1. Defining Containers and Images

Containers and container images are foundational elements of modern software deployment and execution environments. Both play crucial roles in encapsulating software environments and ensuring consistent application behavior across diverse computing environments. This section delves into the fundamental concepts and structures of containers and container images, elucidating their purpose and the technological principles that underpin their widespread adoption.

At its core, a container is a lightweight, standalone, executable software unit that includes everything needed to run a piece of software, such as the code, runtime, system tools, libraries, and settings. Containers are isolated, yet they share the operating system kernel, making them more efficient than traditional virtualization, which requires a complete guest operating system for each virtual machine. The proliferation of container technology is largely credited to these efficiencies, allowing developers and operators to deploy applications across environments seamlessly.

Container images, on the other hand, are static files that encompass the snapshot of a container's environment. These are the building blocks from which containers are instantiated. The container image includes the application binaries, libraries, dependencies, and the configuration necessary to run the application. When a container is launched, it essentially becomes a live instance of its image, inheriting all the predefined settings and components.

To appreciate the full utility of containers and images, it is practical to explore their structure. Container images follow a layered approach, which is integral to their efficiency and flexibility. These layers are stacked in such a way that any existing layer can be reused across different containers, thereby minimizing storage overhead. Every layer in a container image is immutable, which implies that changes to a file

60

within a layer necessitate creating a new layer. Through this method, layers can be shared between images, promoting consistency and saving space.

The Docker containerization model initially popularized the layered file system used in containers, and this concept has been integrated into many containerization tools like Podman, which we will emphasize in this chapter. Each image is derived from a parent image, with distinct layers representing incremental modifications or additions. At the base, there is typically a minimal operating system image layer, purposed to house the necessary commands, utilities, and libraries for an application's execution.

Illustrating with a simple build example, consider the creation of a container image using Podman. Imagine we have a straightforward application written in Python; the following Dockerfile specifies how this image should be structured:

```
# Use a base image with Python installed
FROM python:3.8-slim

# Set the working directory
WORKDIR /app

# Copy the current directory contents into the container at /app
ADD . /app

# Install any needed packages specified in requirements.txt
RUN pip install --no-cache-dir -r requirements.txt

# Make the container's port 80 available to the outside
EXPOSE 80

# Run the application when the container launches
CMD ["python", "app.py"]
```

This Dockerfile is an image specification that comprises several layers, each corresponding to a command. It begins with a base layer (line starting with 'FROM') constituting a Python runtime environment. Followed by a working directory setting, file additions, and dependency installations, each subsequent directive in the Dockerfile forms a new layer atop the preceding one.

An essential aspect of image layer design is optimizing the order and frequency of changing layers. For instance, placing frequently updated files and dependencies towards the later stages of the Dockerfile can aid in leveraging cached intermediate layers during image rebuilds, thereby streamlining development iterations.

Once an image is configured and built from a Dockerfile, utilizing the Podman tool, for example, embraces a simplified command such as:

```
podman build -t my-python-app .
```

Upon executing the above, Podman processes the Dockerfile to generate the container image, assigning it a tag, 'my-python-app' in this case, which simplifies management and retrieval tasks.

Transitioning to the concept of containers — the images provide the template from which containers are instantiated. When a container is initiated, an image is loaded, and users can interact with it using runtime commands such as 'podman run'. Importantly, container runtime ensures process isolation through techniques like namespaces and control groups (cgroups), isolating application processes from each other and the host system, thereby ensuring security and resource governance.

The command below illustrates the execution of a new container from the 'my-python-app' image:

```
podman run -d -p 8080:80 my-python-app
```

This command runs a container in detached mode (backgrounded), mapping host port 8080 to container port 80, priming the application for external interaction. Such port mapping is crucial for network communication, allowing traffic routing between containerized services and external clients.

Containers also facilitate ephemeral characteristics, embodying the non-persistent state by default. This implies any runtime data changes are lost when a container stops. Persistent data needs explicit volume mounts or external storage connectors, ensuring resilience and statefulness when required:

```
podman run -d -p 8080:80 -v /host/path:/container/path my-python-app
```

In the above listing, a volume is mounted at runtime to bridge the host directory '/host/path' with the container path '/container/path'.

The paradigm of containers extends beyond mere application encapsulation. They promote the microservices architecture, where applications are decomposed into loosely coupled services, each running within its isolated container. This decomposition affords scalability, maintainability, and speed in the deployment pipelines, embodying the continuous integration and delivery principles pivotal in DevOps methodologies.

Given the immutable and standardized shipping format, container images simplify dependency management. Developers gain the advantage of assured compatibility across platforms, as containerized applications encapsulate their dependencies. Moreover, the images are self-descriptive; metadata embedded within the images serve as declarative instructions and informational guides.

Considering security, the minimalist scope of a container's operating environment reduces overall attack surfaces. This minimized footprint contrasts traditional virtual machines, where larger, more complex components may present additional vulnerabilities. However, maintaining security integrity demands diligent image management practices, from vulnerability scanning to regular updates and provenance verifications.

Container runtime security encompasses several facets, outrightly involving the safeguarding of userspace processes through kernel security features like SELinux, AppArmor, and mandatory access controls that align with the principle of least privilege. Restrictive capabilities are often imposed upon containers unless explicitly elevated through command-line options.

The microcosm of containers and container images fundamentally transforms how applications are architected, deployed, and operated. They bring forth a modular, platform-agnostic approach that embodies the ethos of scalable and flexible computing environments. Podman, as an emerging tool in containerization, leverages these core principles, amplifying their applicability and ease of incorporation into modern software development and IT operations frameworks. The progression into container orchestration and distributed systems like Kubernetes further emphasizes the role of containers in today's technological landscape, which subsequent sections will explore in deeper contexts.

3.2. Building and Layering Container Images

The process of creating container images is an intricate and essential step in maintaining efficient deployment and execution of applications across various environments. The concept of layering within container images is particularly pivotal, as it serves to optimize storage, enhance modularity, and streamline version management. This section elaborates on the methodologies for building container images, the architecture of layers, and their significant advantages in contributing to the robustness of a container ecosystem.

At a fundamental level, constructing a container image involves defining the environment necessary for the operation of an application, along with any dependencies it requires. This environment is described through a set of instructions encapsulated within a Dockerfile. Utilizing tools such as Podman, these instructions are translated into a structured image, composed of a sequence of layers. Each command in a Dockerfile results in the creation of a new layer, providing incremental improvements or modifications over preceding layers.

Consider an archetypal build scenario, where a Node.js application is to be containerized. A Dockerfile might appear as follows:

```
# Start with a base image
FROM node:14

# Set the working directory
WORKDIR /usr/src/app

# Copy package.json and package-lock.json files
COPY package*.json ./

# Install the application's dependencies
RUN npm install

# Bundle application source
COPY . .

# Specify the port the app binds to
EXPOSE 8080

# Run the application
CMD ["node", "server.js"]
```

In this example, the 'FROM' instruction selects the base image, 'node:14', that contains the essential Node.js runtime. This base layer is critical as it establishes the foundation upon which subsequent layers are added. Additional layers follow, executing instructions such as setting the working directory, copying files, installing dependencies, and ultimately defining the command to run the application.

Every layer in a container image is effectively a layered filesystem where changes are additive. These layers are uniquely identified by a digest, allowing version control and sharing across images or even different projects. When a particular layer has not changed since the last time it was built, it can be "cached" and reused. This feature is a hallmark of efficiency within container image builds, preventing redundant resource utilization.

The procedural efficiency of layering manifests in a critical best practice: arranging the layers so frequently changing components— for instance, application source code—are positioned towards the bottom, with infrequently changing components like system libraries at the top. This ordering ensures only the layers affected by changes incur a rebuild, substantially reducing build times in development cycles.

To create an image from this Dockerfile using Podman, the command executed might be:

```
podman build -t my-node-app .
```

This command invokes the build process, where instructions in the Dockerfile are parsed, and the specified layers are assembled sequentially. Podman encapsulates each new filesystem change within a new layer during this buildup.

Exploring deeper into the structure and strategic layering of container images opens avenues for optimization. For example, leveraging a multi-stage build process can minimize the size of the final image, an important factor when deploying in environments with limited resources or when the speed of data transfer is a priority.

Consider refining the Node.js example with a multi-stage build:

```
# Stage 1: Build the application
FROM node:14 as builder
WORKDIR /app
COPY package*.json ./
RUN npm install
COPY . .
RUN npm run build

# Stage 2: Production image
FROM node:14-slim
WORKDIR /app
COPY --from=builder /app/build ./build
COPY --from=builder /app/node_modules ./node_modules
EXPOSE 8080
```

```
CMD ["node", "build/server.js"]
```

In this Dockerfile, the first stage, 'builder', creates a complete environment for building the application, but the final image utilizes 'node:14-slim' as a much smaller production environment, only copying over the necessary 'build' directory and dependencies from the 'builder' stage. This reduction in image size has performance benefits in terms of reduced download times and improved boot performance.

The concept of layering extends beyond storage optimization, influencing caching of dependencies and build artifacts. By isolating application-specific changes from underlying systems or libraries, dependencies and compiled assets can be cached at an intermediary stage, preventing them from being rebuilt unless absolutely required.

Additionally, layering within container images lends itself to regulatory and compliance advantages. Since layers are read-only, configurations can be locked down, preventing unintended alterations. Furthermore, images can be scanned incrementally to detect and isolate vulnerabilities at individual layers, supporting improved security assessment practices.

Security considerations intertwined with layering necessitate both diligence and strategy. Consistently using base images from trusted sources, applying updates promptly, and implementing layered security controls improve both the resilience and maintainability of container workloads.

Furthermore, strategies such as removing unnecessary packages and tools during the final stages of a build can attenuate the surface exposed to potential vulnerabilities, as can utilizing minimal images designed strictly for production environments.

The integrative technology behind container layering relies on a union filesystem, such as OverlayFS. These filesystems efficiently manage

67

and overlay changes from successive layers, providing the practical un-
derpinnings of layers and the built-in robustness against data redundancy through copy-on-write mechanisms.

In consequence, the process of designing and layering container images is iterative and deeply connected to the application's architecture,
lifecycle, and deployment environment. Best practices in this domain
demand an astute understanding of both software engineering and systems operations, emphasizing harmony between application development, deployment automation, and continuous integration pipelines.

Essentially, layering within container images encapsulates not just the
functional software segments, but also the philosophical approach toward modular, efficient, and reliable software distribution. The underlying principles provide developers and operators with formidable
tools to encapsulate complexity, scale operations, and expand system
capabilities within today's ever-evolving digital ecosystems.

The preceding discussion underscores the irreplaceable role these
methodologies play in modern software landscapes. As we advance,
container orchestration platforms like Kubernetes amalgamate these
concepts, building upon the layered architecture of containers to orchestrate and manage distributed services at scale. Subsequent chapters will detail how these layer-based images are coordinated within
such platforms to realize scalable, reliable, and efficient system architectures deployed within diverse infrastructure environments.

3.3.   Working with Container Registries

Container registries are integral components in the management of
containerized applications, serving as repositories where container images are stored, shared, and distributed across various infrastructure
environments. This section provides an in-depth examination of con-

tainer registries, highlighting their functionality, architecture, and the pivotal role they play in the lifecycle of containerized applications. Understanding these concepts is crucial for effectively deploying, scaling, and managing containers in cloud-native environments.

At a fundamental level, a container registry acts as a centralized storage location for container images. By providing a robust infrastructure for image distribution, registries enable developers and operations teams to push and pull images with ease, facilitating seamless integration into continuous integration and delivery (CI/CD) pipelines. Public registries, like Docker Hub, Red Hat Quay, and Google Container Registry, offer extensive library images, while private registries cater to enterprise needs for customized image management and security.

The architecture of a container registry encompasses several core components: a web API for push and pull requests, a storage back-end, and an authentication mechanism to secure access. Most registries implement the Open Container Initiative (OCI) Image Specification, ensuring interoperability across various container runtime environments, such as Docker, Podman, or Kubernetes.

To interact with a container registry via the command line, developers typically use tools like Podman or Docker. For instance, pushing a container image to a registry involves tagging the image with the registry address followed by an image push operation. Let's consider a typical workflow using Podman:

```
# Tag the image with the registry location
podman tag my-node-app registry.example.com/my-node-app:latest

# Push the tagged image to the specified registry
podman push registry.example.com/my-node-app:latest
```

The command 'podman tag' assigns a tag, which includes the registry address, to the image. The 'latest' tag refers to the current version, a common practice although users can apply semantic versioning (e.g., 'v1.0.0') for clarity. The subsequent 'podman push' command uploads the tagged image to the specified registry location.

Conversely, pulling images from a registry mirrors this process. By specifying the image address, developers can retrieve images efficiently:

```
# Pull the image from the registry
podman pull registry.example.com/my-node-app:latest
```

This command downloads the specified image locally, making it available for instantiation into containers. Container registries optimize this process by employing caching and transfer mechanisms that reduce latency and bandwidth, such as the use of content delivery networks (CDNs) to cache image layers closer to users.

Security is a major consideration when working with container registries. They must ensure the integrity and authenticity of images throughout the distribution process. Registries often enable mechanisms such as Transport Layer Security (TLS) for encrypted communication and secure certificate management to verify image sources. Many registries also incorporate vulnerability scanning, whereby images are analyzed for known security flaws before deployment.

Managing access control is critical to maintaining security. Registries usually incorporate Role-Based Access Control (RBAC) and utilize authentication protocols like OAuth or OpenID Connect. These measures dictate who can push or pull images, providing granular control over image distribution. Consider this example of configuring access permissions:

```
# Create a new role in the registry with restricted access
registry-cli create-role developer --permissions can-read

# Assign the role to a user
registry-cli assign-role --user alice --role developer
```

In this hypothetical registry command-line interface (CLI) scenario, a new role called 'developer' is created, with permissions restricted to reading images only. This role is then assigned to the user 'alice', illustrating how RBAC practices are enforced.

Another crucial aspect of container registries is image version management. As applications evolve, maintaining version history and managing updates proficiently is paramount. Versioned tags, as previously mentioned, facilitate rollbacks or selections of specific image versions. This practice enables developers to track changes over time and revert to known stable states should newer releases exhibit unforeseen issues.

Storage management within registries is optimized through techniques like garbage collection, which removes unused layers from the storage back-end. This action reduces storage footprint and cost, leading to a more efficient use of resources. Additionally, implementing automated policies and alerts can ensure that images are regularly updated and vulnerabilities patched.

Registries can be integrated into CI/CD pipelines to automate the testing and deployment of images. On completion of a successful build stage, an image can be automatically pushed to a registry, triggering subsequent deployment stages. Here's an example snippet from a continuous deployment pipeline configuration:

```
stages:
  - build
  - test
  - deploy

build:
  script:
    - podman build -t my-node-app:${CI_COMMIT_SHA} .

test:
  script:
    - podman run --rm my-node-app:${CI_COMMIT_SHA} npm test

deploy:
  script:
```

```
  - podman login -u $REGISTRY_USER -p $REGISTRY_PASS registry.example.com
  - podman push my-node-app:${CI_COMMIT_SHA}
    registry.example.com/my-node-app:${CI_COMMIT_SHA}
```

In this YAML-based configuration, three stages 'build', 'test', and 'deploy' define the pipeline. The 'deploy' stage pushes the successfully tested image to the registry for deployment.

Finally, container registries form the cornerstone of hybrid and multi-cloud strategies, providing a unified registry interface across diverse cloud platforms. Registries like Amazon Elastic Container Registry (ECR), Azure Container Registry (ACR), and Google Cloud Container Registry (GCR) exemplify the seamless integration of registries into cloud environments, enabling enterprises to deploy containerized applications efficiently across geographically distributed infrastructures.

Container registries are vital to the ecosystem of containerized applications, enabling robust, secure, and efficient image storage and distribution. Proficiency in utilizing container registries, understanding their architecture, and deploying best practices regarding security, access control, and automation greatly enhances an organization's capability to embrace and harness the potential of cloud-native technologies. With the adoption of container orchestration platforms like Kubernetes, the role of registries becomes even more pronounced, as they facilitate the distribution of microservices at scale, further underscoring the importance of mastering these tools for modern software deployment and operations.

3.4. Pulling and Pushing Images to Registries

The process of pulling and pushing container images to and from container registries is a fundamental aspect of the container image life-cycle. This phase involves engaging with registries—repositories that store container images—to facilitate their distribution and deployment across various environments. Understanding these operations is integral to managing containerized applications efficiently within both development workflows and production environments.

Container images are built on local systems and then pushed to a registry. Once stored in the registry, these images are accessible across diverse environments and can be pulled to any system where they need to be instantiated as running containers. This capability is central to the CI/CD pipelines and supports rapid deployment scenarios essential for agile development practices.

- **Pulling Container Images**

Pulling a container image from a registry involves downloading the image from a remote repository to a local environment, where it becomes available to run as a container. This operation ensures that the latest or desired version of an application is readily available for use. The command to pull images typically involves specifying the image repository and tag:

```
# Pulling an image from a registry using Podman
podman pull registry.example.com/my-app:latest
```

This command fetches the image identified by 'my-app:latest' from 'registry.example.com'. The 'latest' tag is a conventional moniker often used to signify the most current stable version of the image, but other tags can denote specific versions or build iterations, employing semantic versioning strategies:

```
# Pull a specific version of an application image
podman pull registry.example.com/my-app:v1.2.0
```

Behind the scenes, the pull operation involves layer-based fetching where only the layers that do not already exist in the local cache are downloaded. This efficiency is achieved by computing a digest hash of each layer to verify its presence. If matching layers are found in the local system, they are reused, thus conserving bandwidth and reducing the time required for image acquisition.

Furthermore, registries can leverage content delivery networks (CDNs) to cache image data at distributed locations, minimizing latency and enhancing the retrieval speed for geographically dispersed users.

- **Pushing Container Images**

After developing, testing, and finalizing a container image locally, the subsequent action is usually to push the image to a remote registry. This task ensures the image is hosted centrally, where it can be managed, versioned, and made available for pulling by other environments or users.

Before pushing an image, it is vital to tag it appropriately with the target registry address. Here is an illustration of tagging and pushing an image using Podman:

```
# Tag an image for the target registry
podman tag local-image:latest registry.example.com/my-app:latest

# Push the tagged image to a remote registry
podman push registry.example.com/my-app:latest
```

The 'podman tag' command modifies the image metadata to include the destination registry, while the 'podman push' command transmits the image. Within this method, only the necessary layers (those not present in the registry) are uploaded, mirroring the efficiency seen in the pull operation.

- **Managing Authentication and Security**

Security is paramount when pulling from or pushing to registries. Most registries necessitate authentication, ensuring that only authorized

74

users can access or modify images. This security layer is typically implemented using username-password pairs, OAuth tokens, or other authentication mechanisms.

To handle authentication with Podman, the following sequence demonstrates logging into a registry prior to executing push or pull operations:

```
# Login to a registry
podman login registry.example.com

# Prompt for username and password
Enter Username: your_username
Enter Password: your_password

# Now push or pull images using authenticated session
```

Here, 'podman login' enables secure communication with the registry by encrypting credentials using TLS and storing them in a configuration file for subsequent operations.

Registries might also enforce layer signing, wherein individual image layers are cryptographically signed. These signatures validate the integrity and provenance of images, ensuring no modifications occur post-publication, significantly mitigating the risk of supply chain attacks.

- **Optimizing Image Sharing**

Efficient image sharing and distribution are pivotal to enhanced deployment pipelines. A key optimization strategy is employing base images that are lightweight and regularly updated. Lightweight images reduce network transfer loads, while updates ensure base layers incorporate the latest security patches and features.

Furthermore, using a shared cache of common base layers across projects or within an organization can cut down on unnecessary downloads, speeding up build processes when repeated dependencies are involved.

Let us consider a tailored strategy for building and distributing images quickly:

```
# Utilize a tiny base image
FROM alpine:3.14

# Install the necessary application dependencies
RUN apk add --no-cache python3 py3-pip

# Copy application code
COPY . /usr/src/app

# Set the work directory
WORKDIR /usr/src/app

# Install Python dependencies
RUN pip install --no-cache-dir -r requirements.txt

# Command for execution
CMD ["python3", "app.py"]
```

The use of the 'alpine' base image keeps the container small, thereby optimizing both storage and transmission.

- **Automating Pipelines**

The integration of image pull and push operations into automated CI/CD pipelines is essential for streamlining the software development lifecycle. In these environments, continuous integration servers build, test, and push images to registries automatically, removing manual intervention and minimizing human error. Let's examine an automated pipeline fragment:

```
stages:
  - build
  - test
  - deploy
```

```
build:
  image: docker:latest
  services:
    - docker:dind
  script:
    - podman build -t my-app:${CI_COMMIT_SHA} .
    - podman tag my-app:${CI_COMMIT_SHA} registry.example.com/my-app:${CI_COMMIT_SHA}

test:
  image: registry.example.com/my-app:${CI_COMMIT_SHA}
  script:
    - podman run --rm registry.example.com/my-app:${CI_COMMIT_SHA} pytest

deploy:
  script:
    - podman login -u $REGISTRY_USER -p $REGISTRY_PASS registry.example.com
    - podman push registry.example.com/my-app:${CI_COMMIT_SHA}
```

The pipeline in question builds a new image with the commit SHA, performs testing using this image in a container, and then pushes the validated image to a registry. By defining the images according to each commit, rollback and audit processes become streamlined, ensuring precise tracking of changes.

3.5. Managing and Tagging Images

The management and tagging of container images are critical tasks in the lifecycle of containerized applications. Proper organization and maintenance of images ensure operational efficiency, mitigate redundancy, and foster dependable deployment strategies across varied environments. This section explores the methodologies for effectively managing container images and delves into the best practices of using image tagging as a powerful version control mechanism.

Image Management Strategies Managing container images involves various tasks, including image organization, cleanup, versioning, and lifecycle policies. The goal is to maintain a lean image repository that supports easy access and retrieval while minimizing resource wastage.

Image Organization and Repositories An organized image repository structure enhances accessibility and traceability. This typically involves segregating images based on development stages, environments, or application modules. Here's an illustration of a logical repository structure:

- **Application Name**
  - **Environment**
    - `my-app/dev/latest`
    - `my-app/staging/v2.0.1`
    - `my-app/production/v2.0.1`

In this structure, separate repositories are defined for development (`dev`), staging, and production, each potentially maintaining various builds (`latest` for the most recent, `v2.0.1` for a specific release).

Image Cleanup Over time, image repositories can accumulate outdated or unused images, consuming unnecessary storage and complicating version management. Image cleanup policies are hence essential to control this growth. These policies might include:

- **Automated Cleanup**: Tools that automate the deletion of images no longer needed. For example, retaining only the last ten builds or those used within a certain timeframe.

- **Garbage Collection**: Registries like Docker Registry offer garbage collection processes that remove unreferenced blobs, freeing up storage space.

For manual image deletion, tools such as Podman provide utilities to remove images locally:

```
# List all images with their IDs
podman images

# Remove a specific image by repository name and tag
podman rmi my-app:old-tag

# Remove an image by ID
podman rmi 2c4ac424d080
```

In this snippet, the `podman images` command lists available images, helping identify those ready for removal. Through `podman rmi`, images can be explicitly deleted using their repository tag or image ID.

Image Versioning Effective versioning practices allow for clear tracking of image updates and changes over time. Utilizing semantic versioning is a common approach, using a format like `MAJOR.MINOR.PATCH`. The semantic version implicates:

- **MAJOR**: Significant changes that are potentially incompatible with previous releases.

- **MINOR**: New, backward-compatible functionality.

- **PATCH**: Backward-compatible bug fixes.

By embedding version numbers in image tags, images can be easily referenced, ensuring coherent environments in both development and production deployments. For instance:

```
# Tagging an image with a semantic version
podman tag local-image:latest my-app:v1.2.3
```

This operation labels the `local-image:latest` image with a versioned tag reflecting its semantic version.

Image Tagging Best Practices   Tagging in container images functions as a pivotal mechanism for identifying, organizing, and deploying specific image builds. Tags offer pointers to image layers, which make them uniquely identifiable and retrievable from registries.

Conventional Tagging Practices   Tags should always represent meaningful snapshot states, aiding developers and maintainers in understanding the image's role or significance. Widely accepted practices include:

- **Using Descriptive Tags**: Tags such as `latest`, `stable`, `development`, or specific version numbers should convey complete information about the image's intended use.

- **Avoiding Overwrites**: Once a tag is pushed to a registry, overwriting it with a different build can lead to deployment inconsistencies. Consistency dictates that tags, once assigned, remain unchanged.

- **Using Build Metadata**: Including build-time metadata like commit hashes provides additional context without altering semantic versioning. This can be expressed as:

```
# Tagging with additional build metadata
podman tag my-app:commit-ed9f3a2 my-app:1.2.3-ed9f3a2
```

The above example shows incorporating a short commit hash into the tag, offering clear traceability back to source control repositories.

Multistage Builds and Minimal Tags   In multistage builds, separating build environments from application runtime environments ensures smaller, more secure images. Only essential components are contained within the final image, reducing size and potential attack surfaces. Here's an illustration of reduced-size tagging:

80

```
# In a Dockerfile defining a multistage build
FROM node:14 AS builder
WORKDIR /app
COPY . .
RUN npm install

FROM node:14-slim
COPY --from=builder /app /app
WORKDIR /app
CMD ["node", "server.js"]

# Building and tagging the image
podman build -t my-app:1.0.0-slim .
```

The node:14-slim base image minimizes the final image size, and the slim tag indicates a lean build, aligning with deployment constraints.

Automating Image Management   CI/CD pipelines automate routine image management tasks, embedding best practices directly into development workflows. Automation enhances repeatability and minimizes human error in managing and deploying images.

Consider integrating an automated tagging step into a build pipeline script:

```
stages:
  - build
  - tag
  - publish

build:
  script:
    - podman build -t my-app:build-${CI_COMMIT_SHA} .

tag:
  script:
    - podman tag my-app:build-${CI_COMMIT_SHA} my-app:latest
    - podman tag my-app:build-${CI_COMMIT_SHA} my-app:v2.0.0-${CI_COMMIT_SHORT_SHA}

publish:
  script:
    - podman login -u $REGISTRY_USER -p $REGISTRY_PASS registry.example.com
```

81

```
- podman push my-app:latest
- podman push my-app:v2.0.0-${CI_COMMIT_SHORT_SHA}
```

Here, each pipeline `build` instance tags the resulting image both as `latest` and with a semantic version/commit combination, after which the `publish` stage pushes the tags to a remote registry. Adopting such strategies within CI/CD pipelines ensures robust version tracking aligned with development commits.

3.6. Understanding Image Formats and Compatibility

Container image formats serve as the foundation for defining, packaging, and transporting containerized applications. With diverse runtime environments and varied deployment scenarios, selecting appropriate image formats and understanding their compatibility is crucial for ensuring seamless integration and execution across platforms. This section delves into the intricacies of container image formats, their structuring principles, and compatibility considerations pertinent to a variety of deployment contexts.

- **Key Image Formats**

The evolution of containerization technologies has led to the establishment of several standards that govern image formats, ensuring interoperability and reliability across different container runtime engines and orchestration systems.

- **Docker Image Format**

One of the earliest and most prevalent formats is the Docker image format, which pioneered the use of layers to efficiently manage image content. Docker images comprise a series of immutable layers, each representing filesystem changes, alongside metadata containing configuration settings.

A typical Docker image's layers are created using commands in a Dockerfile, where each RUN, COPY, or similar instruction generates a new image layer. Such layering, utilizing a union filesystem, allows for both filesystem and storage economies.

Consider this example restructuring from a Dockerfile:

```
FROM ubuntu:20.04

# Install updates and dependencies
RUN apt-get update && apt-get install -y \
    curl \
    apache2

# Copy application files
COPY . /var/www/html/

# Expose the desired port
EXPOSE 80

# Start Apache in the foreground
CMD ["apache2ctl", "-D", "FOREGROUND"]
```

With each instruction, a respective layer is introduced in the image. The "FROM" directive establishes the base, subsequent instructions modify or add new layers, concluding with the "CMD" directive as the configuration metadata instructing the entrypoint command upon container startup.

- **Open Container Initiative (OCI) Format**

The need for a standardized image format to ensure broad interoperability led to the establishment of the Open Container Initiative (OCI). OCI's image specification generalizes the storage and interchange functionalities pioneered by Docker while remaining execution-

83

environment agnostic.

OCI images share much of Docker's conceptual structure, supporting layered filesystem representation. They maintain artifacts including a manifest file, a configuration object, and content-addressable descriptor references to layer data stored as blobs. Compatibility between OCI and Docker images is typically ensured, as OCI-compatible runtimes, such as Podman, naturally integrate with Docker environments.

- **Alternative Formats: Singularity, CRI-O**

While Docker and OCI formats dominate container ecosystems, specialized contexts have fostered unique image formats. Singularity, intended for high-performance computing (HPC), embraces single-file image constructs to circumvent constraints within supercomputing environments. Similarly, CRI-O offers Kubernetes-native image format handling and runtime support through standards-compliant interfaces.

- **Compatibility Considerations**

Compatibility spans multiple dimensions, dictating the efficacy of containerized applications across heterogeneous environments. This includes inter-runtime compatibilities, platform compatibilities, and architectural compatibilities.

- **Inter-Runtime Compatibility**

Running containers ubiquitously across different runtimes necessitates cross-compatible images. Tools like Podman, Docker, and Kubernetes rely on common standards such as the OCI format to maintain interchangeability.

84

Using Podman with OCI or Docker images, for instance, involves minimal steps to handle an image built with Docker:

```
# Pull and run a Docker image using Podman
podman pull docker.io/library/nginx:latest
podman run -d -p 8080:80 nginx
```

The inherent cross-compatibility facilitated by adhering to the OCI spec means Podman seamlessly handles Docker source images, reinforcing deployment flexibility.

- **Platform Compatibility**

Multiplatform support is another leverage provided by evolving image specs. Building images for multiple architecture targets—x86, ARM—extends application reach across diverse device types, from servers to IoT devices.

Utilizing build tools like 'buildx', multi-platform images are crafted in a single build step:

```
# Build multi-platform Docker image
docker buildx build --platform linux/amd64,linux/arm64 -t my-app:
    latest .
```

Such builds compile the result into a manifest list, enabling automated runtime adaptation to the host platform.

- **Architectural Compatibility in Distributed Systems**

In orchestrated environments like Kubernetes, image compatibility extends into specialized orchestrations ensuring consistency across distributed container clusters. Operating constraints such as node architecture or operating system variations necessitate fine-grained control over image builds and deployments. Achieving compatibility translates to architecting images as stateless and immutable, inherently supporting distributed node execution without dependency disparity.

- **Managing Image Updates and Compatibility**

Through lifecycle and versioning practices, containerized systems afford continuous updates without compromising stability across dependencies. Managing updates necessitates routine rebuilding strategies, backward compatibility considerations, and expectations for dependency integrity.

Versioned tagging and semver best practices, detailed in earlier sections, reinforce robust update management. Ensuring backward compatibility, avoiding deprecated instructions, and executing unit or integration tests against newer builds helps preserve system reliability.

Finally, automated pipelines compatible with runtime orchestration frameworks detect configuration drifts and invoke resilient deployment strategies. Kubernetes, supporting compatible image rollouts through manifests, gradual updates, and progressive canary deployments, epitomizes these capabilities:

```
apiVersion: apps/v1
kind: Deployment
metadata:
  name: my-app
spec:
  replicas: 3
  template:
    spec:
      containers:
      - name: my-app-container
        image: registry.example.com/my-app:1.2.0
```

By manifesting a specific image version and replicas, the above deployment automates rollout management across orchestrated environments. This safeguards consistency while promoting adaptability.

Image formats and compatibility lie at the heart of operational coherence within containerized ecosystems. By accommodating standardized and interoperable constructs, developers capably unleash their applications on a vast canvas of computing landscapes. With the continued advancement of multi-cloud and hybrid environments, these principles ensure that software remains portable, adaptable, and resilient, laying the groundwork for future innovations in containerization and beyond. Through judicious management and strategic alignment with the evolving standards, operational success in container management ensures robust and future-proof infrastructure deployments.

Chapter 4

Creating and Managing Containers with Podman

This chapter provides a detailed guide on launching and operating containers using Podman. It covers container lifecycle management, including creation, inspection, interaction, and customization options. Users learn how to handle logging for troubleshooting and manage execution parameters such as environment variables and resource constraints. Additionally, the chapter addresses stopping, restarting, and removing containers efficiently. Through these instructions, readers gain essential skills to effectively utilize Podman for consistent and streamlined container management in their development environments.

4.1. Launching Your First Container

The transition to using containerized environments is greatly facilitated by Podman, a tool that allows users to create, manage, and run
containers as seamlessly as possible. This section focuses on guiding
you through the foundational steps needed to launch your first container with Podman, an essential skill that underpins effective container management in modern development architectures.

Containers package an application's code with its dependencies, providing a consistent environment across different deployments. Podman emerges as a pivotal tool in this domain due to its daemonless
architecture and support for rootless containers, enhancing security
and simplicity.

To initiate your journey with Podman, it is imperative first to ensure a
correct installation. The procedure to install Podman varies based on
your operating system. Below is an example of installing Podman on a
Linux-based system using the command line:

```
sudo apt-get update
sudo apt-get install -y podman
```

Upon installation, it is prudent to verify it by checking the version of
Podman installed. This can be done by executing the following command:

```
podman --version
```

```
podman version 3.4.2
```

The output should display the installed version of Podman, confirming its readiness for use. With Podman set up, the next essential step
is launching your first container. Containers typically run in the background, encapsulating applications while leveraging existing images.

To initiate a new container, you must first identify the appropriate image. The simplest way to retrieve an image is to pull it from a container registry, such as Docker Hub. Consider a scenario where we pull and run an NGINX container, a popular web server. Use the following command:

```
podman pull nginx
```

This command fetches the 'nginx' image from Docker Hub, storing it locally for subsequent use. The process involves:

- Searching for the image in the specified registry.

- Downloading the image layers.

- Storing the image in the local registry.

Having secured the image, you are poised to create and run a container using the image. The following command initializes and starts a new container from the 'nginx' image:

```
podman run -d --name my-nginx -p 8080:80 nginx
```

This command utilizes several options in the context of Podman:

- '-d': This option runs the container in detached mode, allowing the command line to resume activity while the container runs in the background.

- '--name my-nginx': It allocates a user-friendly name to the container, facilitating easy reference in future commands.

- '-p 8080:80': This option maps port 80 of the container to port 8080 on the host machine, allowing external access to the web server via http://localhost:8080.

91

At this juncture, verify that the container is indeed running as antici-
pated. The most straightforward method is to list all the running containers using:

```
podman ps
```

A successful execution displays your newly created 'my-nginx' container, akin to the following output:

```
CONTAINER ID  IMAGE                         COMMAND           CREATED
    STATUS          PORTS             NAMES
c9ae13f20f8e  docker.io/library/nginx:latest   nginx -g 'daemon o…  2 minutes ago
  Up 2 minutes ago  0.0.0.0:8080->80/tcp  my-nginx
```

Accessing the NGINX server via a web browser (http://localhost:8080)
should display the default NGINX landing page, indicating the container is operational and serving requests as intended.

Exploring Rootless Containers in Podman: A notable advantage of Podman over its contemporaries is its capability to operate rootless containers, which run independently of the root user, bolstering security
by minimizing privilege escalation risks. To launch a rootless container
using Podman, ensure that your user is appropriately configured, usually accomplished through a user configuration tool like 'subuid' and
'subgid'.

Here's an example of setting up a rootless configuration:

```
echo "$USER:100000:65536" | sudo tee -a /etc/subuid /etc/subgid
```

The command above sets the user namespace for the rootless container,
crucial for security compliance in environments where root access is
restricted. Post configuration, initiate a rootless container using similar commands as before, without modification, as Podman defaults to
rootless mode when unnecessary.

Understanding Container State and Behavior: Navigating container
operations extends beyond mere execution; understanding their lifecy-

cle management is also essential. With Podman, utilize commands to discern the state of a container, examine logs, and probe running processes. The lifecycle of a container encompasses stages from creation, running, paused, stopped, to removal.

To inspect a container intricately, use:

```
podman inspect my-nginx
```

This command provides a comprehensive JSON manifest detailing the configuration, runtime status, and resource utilization of 'my-nginx', pivotal for diagnostics and resource optimization. The output encapsulates crucial attributes such as network details, state, entry points, and volumes.

Troubleshooting Container Creation: In cases where a container fails to start, scrutinize the logs with:

```
podman logs my-nginx
```

The logs deliver a chronicle of events and errors pertinent to the container, facilitating effective troubleshooting. Further probing of live processes can be accomplished with:

```
podman top my-nginx
```

This command reveals active processes within the container, analogous to the traditional 'ps' command in Unix systems. Such insights empower developers to manage, optimize, and debug container applications aptly.

A critical aspect while working within containers is to manipulate networking aspects as necessary. Podman allows sophisticated networking configurations tailored to mimic complex environments via network creation and management commands.

Launching a container marks the first step towards mastering container management with Podman. The simplicity and flexibility of

93

Podman in orchestrating containers is mirrored in its commands and options, supporting diverse use cases, from simple application deployments to complex, multi-service ecosystems. As you continue to experiment and deploy containers using Podman, you gain intermediary control over applications' environments, ensuring they run reliably and securely across diverse platforms without requiring significant modifications.

Understanding the foundational elements of Podman offers you a robust platform to expand into advanced topics surrounding container orchestration, network administration, and resource management, essential in modern cloud-native applications.

4.2. Container Lifecycle Management

The lifecycle of a container is central to understanding and leveraging the flexibility and power of containerized applications. Managed through Podman's extensive yet intuitive command set, each stage of a container's lifecycle—from creation through execution, pausing, scaling, and eventual termination—serves distinct roles in controlled, reproducible, and isolated application deployment.

The anatomy of a container's lifecycle is characterized by a series of states: Created, Running, Paused, Stopped, and Removed. Each state represents the container's status and the associated set of operations that can be performed. This section expounds on these lifecycle stages, advancing through hands-on examples and elucidating the intrinsic commands that govern these transitions.

Container Creation

The initiation of a container lifecycle begins with its creation. Containers are instantiated from images, which serve as blueprints encapsulat-

94

ing the file system, environment, configurations, and default instructions. The typical command to create a container without starting it immediately is:

```
podman create --name my-container nginx
```

The `podman create` command will configure a new storage layer and return a unique container ID. This ID serves as a pivotal reference point and can be used interchangeably with the container name in subsequent commands. This initial creation phase sets the stage for resource allocation and network configuration, while the container remains in a dormant state.

Running a Container

To transition the container from the Created state to the Running state, the `podman start` command is instrumental. This stage witnesses the container actively executing its processes, with allocated resources actively consumed.

```
podman start my-container
```

Alternatively, you can create and run a container in one seamless command using:

```
podman run --name another-container nginx
```

When the container enters the Running state, it functions as a discrete instance, executing the primary application or command defined in the image's entrypoint or specified during run-time. Inspect containers using:

```
podman ps --filter "status=running"
```

This filters running containers, providing crucial insights into active deployments.

Pausing and Unpausing Containers

The Pause and Unpause states are distinctive, offering transient ceasing of a container's processes without altering its execution state. Pausing is a viable option for short-term resource reallocation or maintenance.

```
podman pause my-container
```

During the Paused state, the container's processes are frozen, halting I/O, compute cycles, and network operations without terminating the existing session. To resume operations, execute:

```
podman unpause my-container
```

Unpausing a container restores it to the state it was in prior to pausing, reinstituting suspended operations seamlessly. Monitoring the paused or unpaused state is feasible using:

```
podman ps --filter "status=paused"
```

Stopping a Container

A more profound intervention in the lifecycle is achieved through stopping, ceasing all processes and freeing allocated resources. While extending beyond a paused state, stopping offers a controlled method to disengage a container.

```
podman stop my-container
```

A stopped container remains in the Stopped state until explicitly removed or restarted. Stopping a container initiates a standard termination sequence, signaling the main process to cleanly withdraw resources and exit.

Restarting a Container

Resuming operations post-halting involves restarting the container, a reversal of the stopping process, reinitiating with original or potentially modified parameters.

```
podman restart my-container
```

Restarting brings a container back to the Running state, preserving previously set configurations while allowing for the resolution of transitory issues by rejuvenating the execution environment.

Removing a Container

The lifecycle concludes with the removal of a container, eradicating all associated data and resources. Carefully exercise such authority, as this action is irreversible and purges all container states beyond recovery.

```
podman rm my-container
```

Executed post-stopping, podman rm provides a clean sweep, expunging the container from the premises, whereas combining removal with force ('-f') can eliminate actively running containers.

Automation and Lifecycle Control

Container lifecycle management extends beyond mere command execution; automation tools and scripts amplify Podman's efficiency. Leverage shell scripts, CI/CD pipelines, and orchestration frameworks to automate lifecycle control, augmenting response times and lowering manual intervention costs.

An illustrative example of a partial automation script:

```
#!/bin/bash

# Check if Podman is installed
if ! command -v podman &> /dev/null
then
    echo "Podman could not be found"
    exit
fi

# Create, run, and manage container lifecycle
container_name="auto-nginx"
image_name="nginx"
```

```
# Create container if it does not exist
if ! podman ps -a --format "{{.Names}}" | grep -w $container_name &>
    /dev/null
then
    podman create --name $container_name $image_name
fi

# Handle lifecycle management
case $1 in
    start)
        podman start $container_name
        ;;
    stop)
        podman stop $container_name
        ;;
    restart)
        podman restart $container_name
        ;;
    remove)
        podman rm $container_name
        ;;
    status)
        podman ps -a --filter "name=$container_name"
        ;;
    *)
        echo "Usage: $0 {start|stop|restart|remove|status}"
        ;;
esac
```

Integrating scripting enhances reliability and predictiveness, yielding substantial benefits in large-scale deployments and microservices architectures.

The lifecycle of containers delineates the continuum of operations from conception to cessation. Mastery of lifecycle management with Podman imparts a refined capability to regulate application ecosystems with precision and reliability. As development and operational landscapes evolve, the agility afforded by containers becomes indispensable, positioning Podman as a key competency for engineering resilient systems in both development and production settings. Empowered by comprehensive lifecycle management, developers and operators can ensure smooth transitions across states, optimizing for performance, resource management, and operational continuity.

4.3. Inspecting and Interacting with Running Containers

Engaging directly with running containers is a crucial skill for troubleshooting, performance tuning, and system monitoring. Podman provides a robust set of tools and commands designed to facilitate inspection and interaction with containerized environments. This comprehensive functionality allows developers and system administrators to access intricate details about the container's execution, resources, and networking while providing mechanisms to interact with processes in real-time.

Inspecting Containers

Inspection involves querying detailed metadata and runtime information about a container. Podman's inspect command supplies extensive, structured output illuminating the inner workings of a container, surpassing surface-level status assessments.

For a direct inspection of a container, use the inspect command as follows:

```
podman inspect my-container
```

The output, formatted in JSON, contains a wealth of details including configuration, state, network settings, and a replicable command string. Understanding this data requires comprehending several key components:

- Config: Includes Image, Cmd, and Env, detailing which image the container originated from, default command executed, and envi-

99

ronment variables set.

- State: Captures running status (Running, Paused), Pid, and StartedAt (timestamp).

- NetworkSettings: Displays IP address assigned, gateway, and exposed ports, essential for network troubleshooting.

- Mounts: Shows mounted volumes resulting in clearer data persistence and volume management understanding.

Extracting individual elements from the JSON output aids specific queries:

```
podman inspect --format '{{.State.Pid}}' my-container
```

This command isolates the process ID (Pid) of the main running command in the container, useful for monitoring and debugging.

Real-time Process Interaction

Engaging with the processes inside a container reflects the operational status and potentially identifies bottlenecks or issues. Use the podman top command:

```
podman top my-container
```

This outputs similar data to the Unix ps command, detailing current processes running within the container, along with CPU and memory usage profiles. Combining this insight with system monitoring utilities yields a comprehensive view of the container's operational health.

Interacting with Container Filesystem

Direct file manipulation within the container expands control over application configuration and diagnostics. Enter the container's environment using podman exec to initiate commands without suspending its primary function:

```
podman exec -it my-container /bin/bash
```

Here, -it forms an interactive terminal session, permitting command execution in real-time. Useful commands in this mode include:

- Examining log files: Use cat or tail to read application logs, elucidating errors or performance degradation points.

- Configuring applications: Edit configuration files or apply temporary settings to test new configurations before persistent implementation.

- Direct environment exploration: Listing directories or verifying the installation status of necessary components to identify configuration discrepancies.

Networking Analysis Using Podman

Analyzing network activity is foundational to ensuring efficient communication and data flow within containerized applications. Podman's inspect and network capabilities provide a grounding point for network analysis, revealing port bindings, IP configurations, and exposed services:

Using inspect for network details:

```
podman inspect --format '{{.NetworkSettings}}' my-container
```

The output provides information such as allocated IP addresses and port mappings, which are crucial for diagnosing connectivity issues or confirming that services are accessible at preferred endpoints.

For interactive network troubleshooting within the container, utilities such as curl, ping, or netstat can be invaluable:

```
podman exec my-container curl -I http://localhost:8080
```

This checks HTTP response headers, verifying service availability within the container's network scope.

Persistent Logs and Application Monitoring

Effective monitoring in containerized environments necessitates deploying persistent logging and analysis strategies to track application behavior over time. Utilize Podman's logging features to access container-specific logs or integrate centralized logging systems.

To obtain logs produced by container applications, utilize:

```
podman logs my-container
```

Furthermore, integrating with logging drivers or systems like ELK Stack or Prometheus enables comprehensive logging from multiple containers, aiding aggregate monitoring and analysis.

For dynamic performance tuning, employ system metric collectors (e.g., top, iostat, vmstat) in tandem with Podman to evaluate resource utilization continuously. Explore scaling opportunities based on in-depth metrics to ensure high availability and fault-tolerance.

Resource Utilization and Limitation

In-depth analysis and successful interaction with running containers rely on proper resource allocation and limits defined prior. Oversee and adjust resource usage (CPU/memory) using:

Resource Querying:

```
podman stats my-container
```

This live-stream resource utilization of my-container, demonstrating dynamic CPU, memory, and network usage.

Resource Limitation during Start-Up:

```
podman run --name limited-container --memory=256m --cpus=1 nginx
```

This line limits the memory allocation to 256 MB and CPU usage to a single core, ensuring resource-sensitive environments remain consistent with performance expectations.

Container Performance Retuning

Reassessing performance tuning settings over time as application needs evolve is critical. Use snapshot assessments through resource inspection commands and real-world operational tests to fine-tune performance characteristics continuously.

Combining Podman with advanced monitoring systems shapes effective alerting strategies and actionable insights contingent upon container-specific metrics. The ability to finely adjust resource allocations, experiment with different configurations, and utilize diagnostic outputs ensures efficacy in adapting dynamic workload demands while preserving resource integrity.

Understanding and operationalizing comprehensive inspection and interactive strategies using Podman heightens introspection into running containers, unlocking deeper insights for performance tuning and operational integrity. By deploying multifaceted approaches encompassing filesystem exploration, network diagnostics, real-time process monitoring, and thorough resource management, developers and operators affirm robust and agile environments conducive to reliable application deployment and sustained operations.

4.4. Customizing Container Execution

Customization of container execution is an essential aspect of deploying containerized applications, offering the ability to tailor container behavior to specific needs. This control encompasses configuring environment variables, setting resource limitations, modifying entry points, and employing volume mounts. Using Podman, all these transformations become easily available, allowing developers and system administrators unprecedented versatility in their deployments.

Environment Variables

Environment variables enable dynamic configuration of application settings within containers. By embedding these within the runtime environment, developers can adjust their applications without altering the underlying code.

To pass environment variables to a Podman container, use the -e or --env flag within the podman run command:

```
podman run --name my-app -e "ENVIRONMENT=production" -e "DEBUG=false"
    nginx
```

In the example above, the application within my-app receives two environment variables: ENVIRONMENT is set to production, and DEBUG is set to false. The container assumes these dynamic configurations as part of its internal environment.

For externally sourced configurations, environment variable files can be more efficient:

```
podman run --name my-app --env-file ./env.list nginx
```

Here, ./env.list includes lines such as:

```
ENVIRONMENT=production
DEBUG=false
```

Resource Constraints

Limiting resources is vital to achieving predictable performance and ensures fair resource allocation across multiple running containers. Podman supports defining constraints on both memory and CPU usage, shielding the host system from potential resource exhaustion by a single container.

Setting memory limits involves the `--memory` flag:

```
podman run --name my-app --memory=512m nginx
```

This limits the container to 512 megabytes of RAM, ensuring that excessive memory consumption does not affect other applications. Similarly, CPU shares can be controlled:

```
podman run --name my-app --cpus=1 nginx
```

This enforces a restriction of a single CPU core for the running container. Collectively, these controls facilitate adherence to quality of service agreements while maintaining application performance and stability.

Custom Entry Points

The entry point determines the default command executed when a container starts. Podman provides flexibility to override the default entry point specified in a container's image, tailoring start-up procedures to align with specific operational requirements.

Customize container startup by employing the `--entrypoint` flag:

```
podman run --name custom-entry --entrypoint "/usr/bin/custom-entry.sh
    " nginx
```

This configuration ensures that `custom-entry.sh` is executed upon initialization, providing the opportunity to establish necessary configuration, log settings, or launch required services that the default configuration might not support.

When combined with command arguments, precise operational modes can be initialized:

```
podman run --name custom-entry --entrypoint "/usr/bin/custom-entry.sh
    " nginx start
```

This example passes start to the script, which can further adapt its behavior based on such inputs.

Volume Management

Volumes play a central role in data persistence beyond the lifecycle of a container, achieving permanence in environments founded on ephemeral architectures. Podman empowers detail-oriented volume specification through mount points, assuring data integrity and persistence independently of the container's lifespan.

Mounting Docker volumes uses the -v flag:

```
podman run --name my-app -v /host/my_data:/container/my_data nginx
```

The -v directive permits binding /host/my_data on the host to /container/my_data within the container.   Data written to /container/my_data is reflected on the host, a pivotal feature for scenarios demanding state continuity across execution cycles and debugging.

Moreover, leveraging tmpfs mounts directly impacts speed and efficiency:

```
podman run --name speedy-app --tmpfs /container/tmp tmpfs-size=64m
    nginx
```

tmpfs mounts, residing in memory, expedite I/O operations, furnishing temporary storage spaces ideal for caching use cases or interim data handling.

Networking Configurations

Networking configuration is paramount for containers to facilitate communication with external services and other containerized applications. Podman accommodates numerous network setups, including port mapping, host networking, and isolated container networking.

Basic port exposure is executed through the -p flag, mapping container service ports to host ports:

```
podman run -d --name web-app -p 8080:80 nginx
```

This maps port 80 within the container to port 8080 on the host, making web services reachable through http://localhost:8080.

Diverging configurations might necessitate the use of a custom network or joining an existing network:

```
podman network create mynetwork
podman run --name container1 --network=mynetwork nginx
```

The above commands create a custom network, mynetwork, to which container1 is attached, fostering separated or cooperative networking environments.

Security Contexts and Isolation

Security in customized container execution spans restrictive mechanisms like user and capability management. Rootless containers naturally elevate security by limiting privileges, but heightened controls are often necessary.

Adjust user permissions directly using:

```
podman run --name secure-app --user 1001:1001 nginx
```

This sets the user and group ID of the initial process within the container, minimizing running code with root privileges.

Additionally, capability assignment authorizes specific kernel operations on a need-to-enable basis:

```
podman run --name scoped-app --cap-add NET_ADMIN --cap-drop SYS_ADMIN
    privileged-image
```

Here, network management capabilities are appended, while general system administration capabilities are negated, relevant for containers serving diverse roles but constrained to certain operational domains.

Execution customization in Podman not only optimizes the performance and security of containerized applications but imbues a tailored, predictable application behavior desired in robust deployment cycles. Whether addressing specific application needs through nuanced environment settings, assuring data persistence via well-managed volumes, or enforcing security constraints, the methods delineated above establish a cohesive approach to enhancing container harmony with deployment intent. Riding the wave of containerized evolution, these customization techniques signify not merely technical mandates but a strategic alignment with broader application architecture overhauls.

4.5. Handling Container Logs

Comprehensive log management is essential for diagnosing issues, monitoring application health, auditing, and ensuring security compliance within containerized environments. Podman offers robust logging capabilities that enable developers and system administrators to efficiently capture, analyze, and manage container logs. This section delves into various techniques to access, interpret, and leverage logs using Podman's command-line utilities, alongside integrating external logging systems for scalable log management solutions.

Access to container logs in Podman is straightforward, utilizing the `podman logs` command. These logs capture standard output (stdout) and standard error (stderr) streams, essential for debugging and operational insights.

To view logs from a specific container, execute:

```
podman logs my-container
```

Specific portions of the logs can be accessed using flags like `--tail` to retrieve the recent entries:

```
podman logs --tail 50 my-container
```

Here, the `--tail` flag restricts the output to the last 50 lines, useful for quick checks on recent events without sifting through potentially verbose logs.

To continuously stream logs in real-time, similar to the `tail -f` command, use the `-f` or `--follow` flag:

```
podman logs -f my-container
```

This continuous feed proves indispensable for developers requiring live feedback during development and testing phases, enhancing the immediacy of reactive debugging and optimization.

Containers often emit unstructured logs, but transitioning to structured logging formats, such as JSON, facilitates parsing, searching, and analysis across distributed systems. Some applications support native JSON logging, which Podman readily captures and outputs.

Suppose an application running inside a container emits JSON logs. The output can be piped to JSON parsers for inline analysis:

```
podman logs my-json-log-container | jq '.'
```

Here, `jq` processes JSON logs, providing pretty-printing, filtering, and transformation capabilities, thus enriching the diagnostic process.

To format and manage logs application-wide, consider integrating log formatting libraries during application development to produce well-structured log records encompassing timestamps, log levels, custom metadata, and transaction IDs.

Effective log management involves implementing rotation and archival strategies to prevent log file growth from consuming excessive storage, especially crucial in environments with limited resource confines. Podman containers can leverage underlying host operating system facilities via log drivers or through manual rotation scripts.

Using a logging driver that supports log rotation ensures that logs are automatically cycled, retaining only recent records to save space, while archived logs remain accessible for historical audits and compliance checks.

Configure log rotation with tools like `logrotate` on the host:

```
/var/lib/containers/storage/overlay-containers/containerID/userdata/
    ctr.log {
    rotate 7
    daily
    compress
    delaycompress
    missingok
}
```

This snippet configures `logrotate` to compress and maintain logs for seven rotations (days) before deletion. Regular audits of these settings ensure efficiency and data availability.

Leveraging logs for troubleshooting involves pinpointing anomalies or correlating errors in logs with application behaviors. Correlation is enriched when logs contain granular timestamps and identifiable metrics tied to log events. Insights into application performance, unexpected behavior, or security incidents often surface from deeply scrutinized logs.

For example, use grep and awk to filter specific error messages:

```
podman logs my-container | grep "ERROR" | awk '{print $1, $3, $5}'
```

This command extracts and formats crucial components from lines labeled "ERROR," isolating pertinent information adorned by specific fields.

To automate alerts based on critical log messages, scripts can bind regex searches to notifications systems, flagging important events to administrators:

```bash
#!/bin/bash

LOGFILE="my-container.log"
tail -Fn0 "$LOGFILE" | \
while read line ; do
    echo "$line" | grep -q "CRITICAL"
    if [ $? = 0 ]
    then
        echo "Critical issue detected: $line"
        # potential email alert command or notification system hook
    fi
done
```

This continuous monitoring script captures key alerts, triggering additional processes or interactions as required.

In scale-intensive environments or where clusters of containers are deployed, centralized logging frameworks offer benefits surpassing localized log handling, promoting consolidated log ingestion, storage, and analysis. Integration with systems like Elastic Stack, Fluentd, or Prometheus streamlines logging across diverse environments.

By configuring Podman to output to these log aggregators, developers achieve enhanced querying, visualization, and correlation capabilities—integral for complex systems' oversight.

An introductory guide to forwarding logs to an Elastic Stack might involve configuring Fluentd as an intermediate agent:

- Install Fluentd on the host or as a dedicated container.

- Use Fluentd input plugins to gather Podman log streams.

- Forward logs via output plugins from Fluentd to Elasticsearch.

Such integration facilitates expansive querying through Kibana dashboards or direct Elasticsearch queries, with built-in alerting frameworks offering real-time insights and notifications.

Logs are vital for security auditing, with unchecked log data posing confidentiality risks. Ensuring secure logging practices in Podman-driven environments demands concerted attention towards:

- Log Rotation: Continually rotate logs to maintain minimalistic data retention strategies.

- Encryption: Adopt encrypted channels for log transmission when centralized systems are involved, safeguarding data integrity.

- Access Control: Set permission boundaries on logs, restricting access solely to authorized personnel or automated systems.

By adhering to these guidelines, logs transform into a fortified resource feeding analytics, compliance, and forensic analyses with integrity.

Effective log management within Podman fosters a responsive and secure operational environment. Emphasizing structured logging, proactive analysis, automation, rotation, and controlled access, developers and operators can deploy informed strategies revolutionizing container oversight. As infrastructures mature and logs proliferate, flexible yet secure handling becomes paramount, forming the backbone of resilient, diagnostic-rich ecosystems.

4.6. Stopping,   Restarting,   and   Removing Containers

Mastery over the lifecycle operations of containers—stopping, restarting, and removing—is vital for maintaining a balanced, efficient, and responsive development and deployment environment. These operations, while straightforward in execution, underpin the dynamic and modular nature of containerized applications managed through Podman. Understanding the nuances involved in each process assists developers and system administrators in gracefully controlling application runtime environments, regulating resource usage, and ensuring a clean state for containerized applications.

Stopping a container involves gracefully terminating its active processes, allowing services to close open connections and write any changes to disk before ceasing operation. This is analogous to executing a shutdown sequence on a running server, where processes are given a chance to terminate cleanly.

The primary command for stopping a container in Podman is:

```
podman stop my-container
```

By default, Podman sends a SIGTERM signal to the main process inside the container, providing it the opportunity to intercept this signal for any cleanup necessary. After a configurable timeout period (defaulting to 10 seconds), a SIGKILL signal is issued to forcibly terminate remaining processes if they have not already exited.

Adjusting the timeout can be achieved via the -t flag, specifying the period (in seconds) Podman waits before forcefully killing the container:

```
podman stop -t 20 my-container
```

This extension offers processes within the container more grace time to conclude, beneficial for applications requiring meticulous shutdown procedures to ensure data integrity or perform closure tasks.

Understanding when to employ a graceful stop versus a forced termination is essential:

- **Graceful Stopping:** Use for containers running stateful applications needing a controlled shutdown to commit transactions or close connections cleanly. For instance, databases or transac-

113

tional services bear significant risks if abruptly halted.

- **Forced Stopping:** Deployed when containers become unresponsive or are immune to termination commands. Leverage podman kill, sending an immediate termination signal:

```
podman kill my-container
```

This procedure results in an immediate stop without affording the container's processes a chance to execute termination handlers, risking data loss or corruption unless proper data layer safeguards exist.

Restarting a container involves stopping it and subsequently starting it anew, known as a soft reboot. Using Podman to restart ensures that resources are reallocated correctly, temporary faults are cleared, and application updates or configuration changes are effectively applied.

The command to restart a container is:

```
podman restart my-container
```

Upon execution, the container receives a stop directive and, after termination, is initiated once more with the original start parameters. This process purges non-persistent states while retaining persistent volumes and environment variables, notably updating images if changes were made and the new image is pulled prior to restart.

Use cases for container restarting include:

- **Configuration Changes:** When environment variables or configurations alter, a restart applies these adjustments, ensuring the application functions with the latest settings.

- **Resource Reallocation:** In dynamic environments, adjusting CPU or memory allocations might be necessary to better distribute host resources among containers. Restarting the container allows these adjustments to take effect.

- **Fault Recovery:** Restarting a container can resolve transient errors like memory leaks, stale connections, or software bugs without requiring a more invasive approach.

Removal purges a container from the system, freeing associated resources, and deleting temporary storage layers. Executing this operation is final; any ephemeral data within the container's storage layers is lost:

```
podman rm my-container
```

A container must be stopped before it can be removed. To remove a running container, combine the -f or --force flag to stop and remove simultaneously:

```
podman rm -f my-container
```

Coupling stop and remove operations in this way is a streamlined approach, particularly useful in build pipelines or cleanup scripts where non-persistent containers are employed for task execution or testing phases.

A provision for automatic removal upon exit salvages resources from containers designed for short-lived or testing purposes. Pass the --rm flag during container initiation to enable auto-removal:

```
podman run --rm --name transient-task-container nginx
```

Such containers dissolve post-process completion, discarding transient data and reducing the administrative overhead entailing removal chores.

Administrators must approach stopping, restarting, and removing containers distinctly and strategically, recognizing implications beyond basic command execution:

- **Avalanches of Operations:** Avoid wholesale concurrent stops or restarts within environments housing interconnected services, deploying rolling changes or orchestrated pauses to prevent system resource contention or service disruption.

- **Resource Optimization:** Through thoughtful lifecycle management policies, administrators conserve host resources and streamline performance by judiciously regulating the count and configuration of running containers.

- **Data Persistence:** Encapsulated data handling strategies through persistent volumes or external storages accentuate secure resource detachment and subsequent container removal.

- **Immutable Infrastructure Practices:** Leveraging container replacement over modification supports immutable infrastructure paradigms, enhancing reliability, and easing A/B testing of differing configurations or software versions.

With Podman, automating container lifecycle operations can be facilitated through scripting or incorporated within orchestration tools (like Kubernetes, OpenShift) that introduce automated restart policies and failure management.

Creating scripts for defined post-execution cleanup or automated restart loops provides a primitive but effective level of automation. Consider a sample script:

```
#!/bin/bash

# Parameters
container_name="batch-job"
image_name="job-image"

# Run job
```

```
podman run --rm --name $container_name $image_name

# Check exit status
if [ $? -ne 0 ]; then
    echo "Error: Job did not complete successfully!"
    exit 1
else
    echo "Success: Job completed!"
fi
```

This ensures jobs encapsulated in containers execute fully and responsibly handle output. In more complex orchestration systems, enhanced control policies automate these steps efficiently.

Harnessing structured capabilities for stopping, restarting, and removing containers through Podman emphasizes robust operational integrity and system efficiency. This management fosters sustainable and scalable growth for containerized applications, allowing developers and operators to enact controlled lifecycles that maximize application resilience, adaptability, and reliability while aligning with strategic long-term architectural goals.

Chapter 5

Container Networking with Podman

This chapter delves into the networking capabilities of Podman, covering the configuration of container network interfaces and port mapping to expose containerized services. It explains DNS settings and service discovery mechanisms, integral for seamless container interaction. Users learn to create and manage custom networks for isolated environments, enhancing control and security. Troubleshooting guidelines address common networking issues, offering solutions for maintaining robust and efficient communication pathways within containerized applications, ensuring reliable performance and connectivity.

5.1. Basic Networking Concepts for Containers

In containerized environments, networking plays a critical role in ensuring communication both within clusters and with external systems.
Understanding how networking operates within a containerized framework, such as Podman, is essential for effective architecture and operation of container-based applications. This section will delve into the
fundamental networking concepts that are particularly relevant to containers.

Containers, by their very design, are lightweight and often ephemeral,
running isolated from the host system. This isolation not only applies
to system resources like CPU and memory but also to networking. Typically, a containerized application will require connectivity to other containers, services, or networks. It is essential to understand how this is
achieved given the constraints imposed by container isolation.

At a foundational level, container networking leverages namespaces,
Virtual Network Interfaces (VNIs), and bridging. Upon the creation of
a container, a dedicated network namespace is established, isolating its
network connectivity from the host and other containers. This ensures
that:

- Packets within the container remain contained unless explicitly
  configured to route elsewhere.

- IP tables and routing tables are specific to each network namespace, allowing fine-grained control over traffic patterns inside
  containers.

Within this isolated namespace, a container typically communicates
through a virtual Ethernet pair. This pair consists of interfaces: one
end is attached to the container, and the other to a Linux bridge on the
host. The bridge acts as a virtual switch, thus enabling communication

between the host and other containers. This is conceptually similar to connecting physical machines to a network using an Ethernet switch.

To examine the configuration of these network namespaces and inter-faces, consider a simple environment setup using Podman. The follow-ing sequence demonstrates how to view network configuration from within a container using Linux commands.

```
$ podman run -it --rm alpine /bin/sh
/ # ip addr show
1: lo: <LOOPBACK,UP,LOWER_UP> mtu 65536 qdisc noqueue state UNKNOWN
    qlen 1000
    link/loopback 00:00:00:00:00:00 brd 00:00:00:00:00:00
    inet 127.0.0.1/8 scope host lo
    valid_lft forever preferred_lft forever
2: eth0@if74: <BROADCAST,MULTICAST,UP,LOWER_UP> mtu 1500 qdisc
    noqueue state UP
    link/ether 02:42:ac:11:00:0b brd ff:ff:ff:ff:ff:ff link-netnsid 0
    inet 172.17.0.2/16 brd 172.17.255.255 scope global eth0
    valid_lft forever preferred_lft forever
```

In the above example, we see that the container is assigned an IP within a private subnet. The use of a private IP space inside containers pro-motes security by segmenting traffic and controlling external access via host-level configurations.

- Network Address Mapping and Routing

One practical necessity is ensuring that containers can communicate with one another and with external entities. This often involves con-figuring Network Address Translation (NAT) on the host to translate requests from the container to an external network and vice versa. The common practice of assigning a single public IP address to the host serving multiple containers is made feasible through NAT.

The function of NAT within container ecosystems primarily falls under two categories:

- Source NAT (SNAT): Alters the source address of packets origi-

121

nating from the container for external routing.

- Destination NAT (DNAT): Commonly used for port forwarding, altering the destination address of incoming requests to map to the appropriate container's IP and port.

Podman's default networking employs setup scripts to handle typical scenarios automatically, bridging containers via a common network and translating network packets as needed. However, there are scenarios where custom network setups offer enhanced security and functionality. To accommodate these requirements, understanding the roles of SNAT and DNAT operations is essential.

```
# Example of optional iptables rule for SNAT
$ iptables -t nat -A POSTROUTING -s 172.17.0.0/16 -o eth0 -j
    MASQUERADE

# Example DNAT rule mapping host's port 8080 to a container's web
    server port 80
$ iptables -t nat -A PREROUTING -p tcp --dport 8080 -j DNAT --to-
    destination 172.17.0.2:80
```

- Network Models

The container networking model can be extended to customize how these network interfaces interact, using a variety of network drivers available within container orchestration systems, such as bridge, host, overlay, and none. Understanding these models enables decisions on isolation, performance, and resource utilization.

- Bridge Networks: The default and most common setup. Containers are connected to a host-level bridge for routing. It provides isolation from host processes and can be efficiently scaled.

- Host Networks: Bypasses network namespace isolation for cases where lowest latency is required. Containers share the host's network stack and interfaces, permitting more direct access but sacrificing some isolation.

- Overlay Networks: Useful in orchestration contexts, spanning multiple hosts. Overlays enable inter-container communication across nodes in a cluster and involve significant complexity involving encapsulation techniques such as VXLAN.

- None: Disables networking for isolated compute environments where networking isn't needed or desired.

- DNS and Service Discovery

DNS and service discovery within container networks are pivotal for enabling communication without hard-coding IP addresses. Containers often require dynamic IP allocation during scaling operations, thus DNS enables seamless interaction by resolving service names to current IP addresses or aliases configured at runtime.

Podman, like many container runtimes, provides internal DNS services. It handles name resolution between containers and can interact with external DNS services.

```
# Inspect the internal DNS settings of a container
$ podman inspect --format '{{ .NetworkSettings.DNS }}' <
    container_name>
```

Lastly, an important aspect of container communication is service discovery. Service discovery can be automatic, leveraging DNS, or manual configuration files, based on the complexity and requirements of the deployment.

- Container Network Security

Security is paramount in any networking model, especially in containerized environments. Network isolation, firewall rules, and limited ports exposure through DNAT play key roles in securing container communication pathways. Implementing the principle of least privilege and ensuring containers have access only to necessary resources are best practices.

Firewalls and security groups positioned in host or cloud-level environments can enforce policy on container traffic, ensuring that only authorized container-to-container and container-to-external communications occur.

Using multi-stage containers to specialize roles—segregating, for example, a container's database operations from network-facing web services—enhances security management by compartmentalizing responsibilities and reducing potential attack surfaces.

In summary, understanding basic networking concepts for containers involves learning how network namespaces, NAT, network models, and security features integrate to provide robust and efficient communications while maintaining container isolation. Through declarative networking configurations, orchestrators like Kubernetes can manage complex networking setups, thus automating much of the deployment process. The principles discussed here lay a foundation for more advanced networking topics and their practical implementation using container tools such as Podman.

5.2. Configuring Container Network Interfaces

Configuring network interfaces within containers is a central task for ensuring that containerized applications can communicate effectively with other applications and services. This section delves into how network interfaces are set up and managed within containerized environments using Podman, offering insights into the techniques and tools used to configure them.

Containers are typically assigned one or more network interfaces dynamically managed by the container runtime. These interfaces often consist of a combination of virtual Ethernet pairs and network bridges, enabling network traffic to be effectively routed within a containerized host environment and beyond. This setup is crucial for maintaining a functional and interconnected container ecosystem.

- **Understanding Network Interface Creation**

When a container is instantiated, Podman, like other container runtimes, automatically assigns it virtual network interfaces. These interfaces are created as part of a default network namespace that isolates the container's networking environment. This isolation ensures that the container operates within its own secure network space, distinct from both other containers and the host system, enforcing security and preventing unintended interactions.

A fundamental understanding of container network interfaces begins with grasping how these interfaces are created and configured. When a new container instance is launched, Podman generates a pair of virtual Ethernet devices (veth). One end of this pair is attached to the container network namespace, and the other end is attached to a Linux bridge on the host.

This bridging provides the necessary mechanism to relay network traffic between the container and the external network. This configuration can be outlined by examining the virtual Ethernet setup. Consider a sample execution where the container interface settings are queried:

```
$ podman run -it --rm alpine /bin/sh
/ # ip link show
1: lo: <LOOPBACK,UP,LOWER_UP> mtu 65536 qdisc noqueue state UNKNOWN
    mode DEFAULT group default qlen 1000
    link/loopback 00:00:00:00:00:00 brd 00:00:00:00:00:00
2: eth0@if234: <BROADCAST,MULTICAST,UP,LOWER_UP> mtu 1500 qdisc
    noqueue state UP mode DEFAULT group default
    link/ether 02:42:ac:11:00:1f brd ff:ff:ff:ff:ff:ff
```

This snippet illustrates the presence of 'eth0', a typical Ethernet interface within the container. The configuration permits communication outwards via the host's network bridge.

• Customizing Network Interfaces with Podman

Podman provides mechanisms to alter network interface configurations to suit specific networking requirements. This customization allows changes to be made to IP address allocations, subnet partitions, and even interface MTU settings. The choice of networking mode and configuration depends heavily on the application needs and the desired security posture.

Modification often begins with defining custom networks. By default, Podman uses the 'cni' (Container Network Interface) plugin settings for IP assignment. However, developers can define custom configurations through the 'podman network' command suite. For instance:

```
$ podman network create --subnet=192.168.100.0/24 mycustomnetwork
```

This command creates a new network named 'mycustomnetwork' with a specified subnet range, effectively isolating traffic to this defined network segment. Containers using this network will thus receive IP addresses within the '192.168.100.0/24' network. It's crucial to note that Podman networks are flexible and support multiple networks with overlapping subnets by maintaining strict namespace isolation.

• IP Management and Hostname Resolution

Podman's network settings can be tailored to configure static IP addresses and customize DNS resolution tactics within containers—essential capabilities for microservices architectures that require predictable networking configurations.

126

Assigning a fixed IP address to a network interface within a container involves specifying options during container instantiation. Consider launching a container with a static IP:

```
$ podman run --network mycustomnetwork --ip 192.168.100.10 -d nginx
```

The above command runs an 'nginx' server within the 'mycustomnetwork', pinned to IP '192.168.100.10'. This predictability is beneficial in configurations where containers interact with external services expecting consistent addressing.

Furthermore, internal DNS services are customizable per container and network through Podman configuration, using both static and dynamically assigned DNS servers. This adaptability aids service discovery, crucial in container deployments spanning multiple networks.

```
$ podman run --network=mycustomnetwork --dns=8.8.8.8 -d alpine sleep
    3600
```

This example launches a container in 'mycustomnetwork' using Google's DNS service for resolutions, showcasing how to bypass default configurations. As command-line options might not always suffice, these DNS settings can also be defined in detailed network configuration files for enterprise-level deployments.

- **Persistent Interface Configuration**

For scenarios necessitating persistent changes across container reboots, additional configuration management utilizing network plugins or third-party tools might be necessary. Persisting configurations ensures uniformity across deployments, enhancing debugging and management.

Podman supports editing the bridge interface configurations via its CNI setup. These configurations are typically located in the CNI configuration directory and can be adjusted to reflect persistent changes to network bridges:

```
{
  "cniVersion": "0.4.0",
  "name": "mybridge",
  "type": "bridge",
  "bridge": "cni0",
  "isGateway": true,
  "ipMasq": true,
  "ipam": {
    "type": "host-local",
    "subnet": "10.88.0.0/16",
    "routes": [
      { "dst": "0.0.0.0/0" }
    ]
  }
}
```

This JSON example outlines a simple 'bridge' configuration file for a CNI-compliant interface, defining IP addressing and gateway settings. Configurations from such files are applied at runtime, ensuring consistency across containers that leverage these interfaces.

- **Security Implications and Best Practices**

Configurational control over network interfaces within containers extends beyond functionality into security. Ensuring that containers are configured with the principle of least privilege is essential in minimizing potential attack vectors.

- Isolated Network Controls: When configuring interfaces, segregated networks prevent unnecessary exposure of services, crucial in distributed environments.

- Immutable Network States: Utilizing read-only network configurations for critical services reduces risk from dynamic exploits.

- Interface Rate Limiting: Implementing network rate limiting can thwart denial-of-service vectors, preserving service availability.

Moreover, monitoring tools can be integrated into Podman environments, ensuring configurations align with security best practices and compliance benchmarks.

- **Advanced Interface Features**

For advanced orchestration needs, interface management might include VLAN tagging, QoS policy enforcement, and eBPF (extended Berkeley Packet Filter) utilization for networking stack enhancements. Podman, through its flexible networking designs, permits such integrations to supplement native capabilities.

By leveraging additional points such as ingress, mesh networks, or SDN controllers, Podman's scope can extend beyond basic container interactions. Such configurations are frequently orchestrated through supplementary tools like Network Policy Managers, which define and enforce policy across diverse network layers.

In essence, configuring container network interfaces involves a thorough understanding of the networking fabric of container runtimes. Podman provides a robust set of tools and options for creating, modifying, and managing network interfaces effectively. The ability to adapt configurations specifically to meet complex application requirements continues to drive greater adoption and integration of containers into modern cloud architectures.

5.3. Port Mapping and Exposing Container Services

Port mapping is a fundamental concept within container environments that allows external access to services running inside a container. Understanding and configuring port mappings correctly is pivotal for ensuring that containerized applications can be accessed from outside their isolated network environment, providing the necessary bridge between internal operations and external clients.

In containerized architectures, applications usually run in isolated containers without inherent connectivity to external networks. This isolation, while beneficial for security and resource management, poses a challenge when services need to be exposed to users or systems outside the container ecosystem. Port mapping resolves this by binding ports from the container's running application to ports on the host machine, allowing external entities to communicate with the service.

Port Mapping Fundamentals

When a container is started, it often runs a service such as an HTTP server, database, or proprietary application. These services listen on specific ports. The container runtime, like Podman, facilitates communications between the host and the container by mapping these specific container ports to available host ports.

Container ports are internal, and the service binds to these ports typically within the container network namespace. For communication from outside this namespace, Podman directs traffic from a specified host port to the container port using Network Address Translation (NAT).

Podman makes port mapping intuitive with command-line configurations, providing an instantaneous method to expose services. For instance, consider an HTTP service listening on port 80 within a container. To map this container port to host port 8080, you would use:

```
$ podman run -d -p 8080:80 nginx
```

In this command:

- -d runs the container in detached mode.

- -p 8080:80 specifies the host port 8080 is mapped to the container port 80.

This binding allows incoming HTTP requests on `http://<host_ip>:8080` to be forwarded to the service running inside the container on port 80.

Dynamic and Static Port Binding

A significant aspect of port mapping is deciding between dynamic and static port binding. Dynamic binding, where the host port is randomly assigned at runtime, offers flexibility and reduces port conflicts between multiple concurrently running containers. Static binding, as demonstrated above, binds a specific container port to a predefined host port, ensuring predictability and is crucial for service level agreements (SLAs) and specific client communication.

To assign a dynamic port mapping, you might use:

```
$ podman run -d -p 8080 nginx
```

Here, the omission of specifying a container port causes Podman to apply any first open port within the ephemeral range on the host. While beneficial in development environments, dynamic mappings necessitate mechanisms like service discovery to inform potential clients of the mapped port.

Multiple Port Mappings

Applications that utilize multiple protocols or serve diverse types of requests may require multiple port mappings. This is especially common with microservices that handle HTTP, HTTPS, and other protocols.

Consider an application served over both HTTP (port 80) and HTTPS (port 443) within a container. The typical Podman command to expose both services is:

```
$ podman run -d -p 8080:80 -p 8443:443 mywebservice
```

131

Both 8080 and 8443 represent host ports, providing externally accessible endpoints to the service's HTTP and HTTPS interfaces, respectively. These mappings ensure fault-tolerant and redundant external access modes for web applications in production environments.

Understanding Host Network Interfaces

Port mapping is not only applicable for external Internet or intranet access but also allows fine control over which host network interfaces are exposed to incoming connections. Administrators can bind ports to specific network interfaces using IP addresses in the -p flag.

Binding a container's HTTP service to a specific host IP address, for example, is executed as:

```
$ podman run -d -p 192.168.1.100:8080:80 nginx
```

With this command, only clients within the subnet that can directly reach 192.168.1.100 can access the containerized service. This technique provides granular control over network accessibility, crucial for services restricted to intranet consumption or for load balancing among a series of network-facing hosts.

Security Considerations in Port Mapping

Exposing containerized services comes with security implications that necessitate attention to detail. Most prominently, minimizing the attack surface by ensuring no unnecessary ports are mapped and exposed is a best practice.

Additionally, using firewall rules to govern these mapped ports' accessibility enhances security:

```
# Example iptables rule to limit access to exposed port
$ iptables -A INPUT -p tcp --dport 8080 -j ACCEPT
$ iptables -A INPUT -p tcp --dport 8080 -s 192.168.1.0/24 -j ACCEPT
$ iptables -A INPUT -p tcp --dport 8080 -j DROP
```

These rules restrict access to the mapped 8080 port only for clients within the 192.168.1.0/24 subnet, dropping all other inbound connections.

Moreover, leveraging TLS for secure communication on exposed ports, especially for HTTP-based services, mitigates risks associated with unencrypted data transmission. Adding security headers, managing proper secrets for automated authorization, and routinely auditing exposed services further improve the container's security posture.

Monitoring and Auditing Port Mappings

Port mapping, while straightforward, may invite unexpected issues like port conflicts and unauthorized access. Continuous monitoring of port mappings is vital to trace network flows, diagnose issues, and ensure compliance with security policies.

Podman provides introspection capabilities to review currently active port mappings:

```
$ podman port <container_id>
```

This command lists all the port bindings for a particular container, facilitating quick insights into which ports are currently exposed and through which host interfaces they are accessible. This data aids in troubleshooting connectivity issues and validating desired configurations.

In conjunction with Podman's capabilities, using network monitoring tools like Prometheus and Grafana to visualize traffic metrics across mapped ports can be insightful. These tools can be linked into CI/CD workflows to ensure cloud-native applications maintain optimal and secure configurations autonomously.

Advanced Port Mapping in Container Orchestration

Within orchestrated environments like Kubernetes, port mappings

133

may be abstracted or implemented at a more sophisticated level through techniques such as Ingress Controllers, which offer rich layer 7 routing and scaling capabilities. Kubernetes facilitates the concept of Services and Ingress Resources for managing exposure, granting a centralized mechanism to manage access controls, load balancing, and SSL termination, consolidating operational overhead traditionally managed through individual container configurations.

Podman can integrate with Kubernetes, thanks to compatibility and containerization standards, via containers as part of Kubernetes Pods defined with YAML configurations, enhancing composability and operational consistency.

Deftly managing port mappings and exposing container services effectively translates containerized application functionality to the broader internet or networked environments. This technique remains an integral element of provisioning, maintaining service availability, and ensuring a scalable architecture. By mastering port mappings, administrators can efficiently deliver container services with assured accessibility and robust security enforcement.

5.4. DNS and Discovery in Container Networks

Domain Name System (DNS) and service discovery are pivotal mechanisms within container networks, enabling seamless and dynamic interaction between containerized services. When deploying applications across distributed container environments, the ability to resolve, locate, and interact with services dynamically assumes paramount importance, necessitating a comprehensive understanding of how DNS and discovery services are configured and operated within containerized ecosystems.

Understanding DNS in Container Contexts

DNS within containerized environments plays a crucial role in mapping service names to IP addresses. Given that containers are often ephemeral and can be frequently redeployed, relying on static IPs becomes infeasible. Instead, DNS provides a dynamic approach to accessing containerized services by using logical, human-readable names.

In a standard configuration, a container is provisioned with DNS settings that enable it to resolve both internal service addresses and external domain names. This dual capability is facilitated by the running container engine, like Podman, which handles the DNS configuration transparently for standalone containers.

When a container is instantiated, Podman configures DNS resolution by inserting entries in '/etc/resolv.conf' within the container namespace, specifying the name servers it will use. These entries can be modified or extended to incorporate custom DNS needs, allowing containers to communicate across diverse networks effectively.

Configuring DNS for Containers

Configuring DNS for containerized applications can involve specifying DNS servers, search domains, and other resolver settings. For Podman, this configuration can be accomplished at container runtime.

An example command implementing custom DNS settings in Podman might appear as:

```
$ podman run -d --name mycontainer --dns=1.1.1.1 --dns-search=example
  .com nginx
```

Here:

- --dns=1.1.1.1 specifies a custom primary DNS server for the container, in this case, Cloudflare's DNS service.

- --dns-search=example.com adds a custom DNS search domain, aiding in the resolution of intra-network service names.

These options override default configurations, enabling scenarios such as testing deployment against different DNS infrastructures or introducing localized DNS routing.

Internal DNS Service

Podman and other container orchestrators, such as Kubernetes, often natively provide internal DNS capabilities, automatically managing the resolution of services within the same cluster or defined network space. This progression is crucial for microservices architectures that rely upon the rapid scaling and dynamic reassignment of resources.

For instance, in Kubernetes, a DNS server runs as a service, translating service names defined in the Kubernetes API to IP addresses and providing seamless interaction between pods and services. Podman can complement this by providing DNS settings that align with the libpod specifications for container communications.

DNS-Based Service Discovery

Service discovery is an automated process that enables containers to discover and connect to services within the network. In dynamic environments where services might start and stop or relocate frequently, discovery systems help maintain functionality by directing service consumers to current service addresses or instances.

There are two principal models of service discovery often discussed in the context of containerized environments:

1. Client-Side Discovery: Here, the client is responsible for querying the service registry to fetch available instances. The application often contains logic to locate the registry and select a service instance from a list.

2. Server-Side Discovery: Contrarily, a load balancer between the client and service holds the responsibilities. The client requests

the service via the load balancer, which proxies and routes the request to an active service instance.

In a Podman-centric container setup, service discovery can be orchestrated using DNS, configuring internal DNS servers or integrating service registries such as Consul or etcd to maintain service entries.

Exploring Service Discovery with DNS

An exemplary system using DNS for service discovery might operate with the help of SRV records, which map service protocol operations to their respective network addresses and ports. SRV records in DNS are essential for managing network service handling due to their ability to dynamically respond with service-specific information.

Consider a scenario with multiple instances of a web service running behind a DNS-based load balanced configuration among containers:

```
$ podman run -d --name web1 --dns=10.1.1.1 mywebserver
$ podman run -d --name web2 --dns=10.1.1.1 mywebserver
```

Assuming an internal DNS server configuration that includes corresponding SRV records for these services, the DNS query for `_http._tcp.webservice.example.com` might dynamically resolve to one or several service instances, such as 'web1' or 'web2', informing client applications where to direct HTTP requests.

Advanced Considerations and Integration

DNS and service discovery integration can evolve into sophisticated configurations, accommodating scaling requirements, enforcing strict network policies, or integrating with federated DNS systems. Leveraging features like DNSSEC can bolster the trust in DNS responses, ensuring responses are authentic and untampered.

Podman users might opt for implementing external DNS and discovery solutions, closely aligning container networks with tools like CoreDNS, enhancing flexibility and configurability. CoreDNS provides modular architectures with plugins, extending standard DNS capabilities, fitting seamlessly within CI/CD pipelines for automated configuration updates and real-time service scaling.

Security Implications and Best Practices

Deploying robust DNS and discovery setups necessitates rigorous attention to security practices:

- DNS Security Extensions (DNSSEC): Ensure that DNS responses are authenticated and have not been compromised en route, reducing risks of DNS spoofing and cache poisoning.

- Network Policy Management: Implement network policies within orchestrators to control which services or clients can communicate, enforcing logical boundaries between network segments.

- Service Mesh Integrations: Employ service meshes such as Istio to manage service discovery at scale, implementing mutual TLS (mTLS) and tracing for enhanced observability and security.

Monitoring and Troubleshooting DNS

Monitoring DNS performance and ensuring service discovery health are crucial for maintaining network reliability. Tools like Prometheus, Grafana, and Jaeger can be employed to trace DNS queries, detect latency issues, and optimize service routing effectively.

Moreover, Podman's command utilities such as `podman inspect` and `podman logs` can be leveraged to debug DNS settings and service communication pathways, identifying configurations that require rectifying to ensure service discoverability and reduce latency.

5.5. Creating Custom Networks for Containers

Creating custom networks is a fundamental aspect of effectively managing containerized environments. Custom networks allow for isolation, security, and optimized performance of container applications. By creating controlled network environments tailored to application requirements, administrators can ensure robust communication between containers and networks. This section will explore the process of setting up and managing custom networks using Podman.

Conceptual Overview of Custom Networks

Custom network configurations within container environments provide the ability to enforce network policies, enhance security, limit communication to necessary services, and optimize resource usage efficiently. In essence, a custom network is a virtualized environment that containers use to communicate within a specified boundary. These networks can span multiple containers on a single host or across multiple hosts, depending on the deployment's scope and complexity.

Within Podman, as with other container runtimes, the default network settings suffice for many simple applications. However, as the deployment grows in complexity, tracking interactions, defining ingress/egress rules, and managing resources dictate the use of custom networks.

Benefits of Custom Networks

- **Isolation**: Custom networks allow isolation of application components, limiting interaction only between containers that need to communicate. Ensuring certain services can only be accessed by specific parts of an architecture reduces possible security vulnerabilities.

- **Security**: By restricting exposure to internal services, applica-

tion security is enhanced. Custom networks support the application of firewall rules, encryption standards, and other security
controls that are critical for protecting sensitive data and services.

- **Scalability and Performance Optimization**: Networks can
be tailored to maximize bandwidth, minimize latency, and optimize connections based on workload needs. This setup is particularly important for microservices and distributed systems, where
network performance significantly impacts overall application efficiency.

Creating a Custom Network in Podman

Podman simplifies the process of creating custom networks through its
command-line interface. Using the 'podman network' command, users
can define networks that hold specific settings for container intercon-
nectivity.

To create a new network, the general command is:

```
$ podman network create mycustomnetwork
```

This command generates a new network called 'mycustomnetwork'.
Containers connected to this network can communicate with each
other directly, but are by default isolated from containers on other networks unless additional routing is defined.

Configuring Network Parameters

When creating a custom network, nuanced configuration options allow
specifying subnet ranges, gateway addresses, and DNS settings. These
parameters dictate how containers will interact internally and with the
outside world.

Consider an example:

```
$ podman network create --subnet=192.168.10.0/24 --gateway
  =192.168.10.1 --dns=8.8.8.8 mycustomnetwork
```

This command sets:

- A subnet of '192.168.10.0/24', providing IP addresses for containers on this network.

- A default gateway of '192.168.10.1', managing outgoing traffic to other networks, including public internet access.

- Custom DNS server '8.8.8.8', setting external DNS resolution capabilities for containers.

Advanced Networking Features

Incorporating advanced networking features into custom networks enables fine-tuned control over network traffic and interactions between services. Podman supports extensions like VLAN tagging for network segmentation and traffic prioritization through QoS (Quality of Service).

Network Isolation Techniques

Securing container networks often incorporates using private subnets, stringent IP Tables configurations, and ingress controls. Deploying ingress controllers, specially configured firewalls, and proxy services ensures that only vetted traffic can access or exit the network.

Deploying isolated networks can also mean leveraging user-defined IP ranges and only exposing necessary endpoints. Consider:

```
$ podman network create --subnet=10.0.0.0/24 isolated_net
$ podman run --network=isolated_net an_app_needing_isolation
```

Here, providing an isolated network ensures that traffic does not intermix with other less-protected services.

141

Inter-Container Communication

Interconnecting containers across custom networks might require bridging techniques, where container-to-container communication spans multiple custom networks. This complexity can be handled by setting up routing rules through Environment-Specific IP settings and carefully planned CIDR blocks.

Real-World Application and Integration

Custom networks serve as the backbone for more sophisticated container orchestration and management systems. Platforms like Kubernetes automate custom network configurations through plugins like Calico, Contiv, and Weave Net, offering advanced networking capabilities overlaid across clusters.

In Podman, orchestration can leverage systemd or Kubernetes CRI (Container Runtime Interface) to manage large-scale networks with similar sophistication, using Ansible or Helm Charts for deployment automation.

An essential aspect of these setups also involves integrating with CI/CD pipelines where network configurations dynamically adjust based on deployed stages testing, staging, or production.

Security Considerations

Custom networks improve security but also require vigilant monitoring and policy enforcement. Leveraging network policies to restrict access in and out of individual containers or application layers protects against both internal and external threats. Network encryption, enforced via TLS, and regular audits ensure adherence to security compliance standards.

Network policies might look like:

```
$ iptables -A FORWARD -i <network_interface> -j DROP
```

The 'iptables' rule above closes unintended traffic paths, ensuring packets respect intended network flows.

Monitoring and Management

Implementing robust monitoring solutions, including integration of monitoring tools like Prometheus with Grafana dashboards, allows for visibility into network traffic patterns, potential bottlenecks, and misconfigurations.

Podman provides network inspection abilities:

```
$ podman network inspect mycustomnetwork
```

This introspection aids in verifying current configurations or iterating new requirement-driven configurations.

5.6. Troubleshooting Container Networking Issues

In container environments, networking issues can pose significant challenges that impact application performance, connectivity, and reliability. Troubleshooting these issues effectively requires a structured approach to diagnosing problems, understanding common failure points, and applying targeted solutions. This section provides a comprehensive guide to identifying and resolving networking issues in containerized setups using Podman, offering practical techniques and tools to maintain optimal network functionality.

- **Common Networking Issues in Containers**

Networking problems in container environments can manifest in various forms, including:

- Connectivity Failures: Containers unable to communicate internally or with external networks.

- DNS Resolution Problems: Failure in resolving hostname, often due to misconfigured or inaccessible DNS servers.

- Latency and Performance Degradation: Network traffic delaying communication between containers and services.

- Port Conflicts: Overlapping or incorrectly mapped ports leading to access issues.

- Security Misconfigurations: Exposed ports or unauthorized traffic compromising network integrity.

Understanding these common issues provides a foundation for effective troubleshooting and resolution.

- **Initial Diagnostic Steps**

When investigating container networking issues, initial diagnostic steps involve verifying that basic configurations and settings are correct. This includes checking network configurations, verifying connectivity, and evaluating container status.

- Checking Network Configurations

Start by inspecting the network settings within the container to ensure they align with expected parameters. Use Podman's command-line tools to retrieve configuration data:

```
$ podman network inspect <network_name>
```

Review the output for subnet information, gateway settings, and connected containers. Confirm that each container's IP aligns with the expected address range.

For individual container network settings, use:

```
$ podman inspect --format "{{ .NetworkSettings }}" <container_id>
```

This command returns network details specific to the container, including IP addresses, DNS servers, and port mappings.

- Verifying Connectivity

Testing network connectivity helps determine if the issue lies in the pathway between containers or external networks. The 'ping' and 'curl' commands provide basic tests for reachability and HTTP services verification:

```
$ podman exec <container_name> ping -c 4 <target_ip>
$ podman exec <container_name> curl http://<target_address>:<port>
```

Use these commands to validate both internal and external connectivity, ensuring the container can access necessary services.

- Addressing DNS Resolution Issues

DNS resolution problems can lead to failures in service discovery and communication between containerized applications. Ensuring correct DNS setup is crucial for maintaining smooth operation.

- Verifying DNS Configuration

Inspect the DNS configuration within containers by examining the contents of /etc/resolv.conf:

```
$ podman exec <container_name> cat /etc/resolv.conf
```

Ensure that the DNS entries reflect the expected servers and search domains. Misconfigured or unavailable DNS entries necessitate corrections either via container runtime options or network configuration files.

145

If custom DNS servers are required, run the container with:

```
$ podman run --dns <dns_server> <container_image>
```

Correct DNS entries prevent lookup failures that can stall service communication.

- Resolving Port Conflicts and Exposures

Port conflicts arise when multiple services attempt to bind to the same port on a host. Resolving these issues requires understanding and verifying the current port mappings.

- Inspecting Port Mappings

Use Podman to inspect containers for conflicting host ports:

```
$ podman port <container_id>
```

The command lists port bindings, helping identify overlaps. Adjust configurations to use unique host ports if conflicts are detected.

```
$ podman run -d -p <available_port>:<container_port> <container_image
    >
```

Change `<available_port>` to resolve conflicts, ensuring exclusive host ports for each service.

- Security Implications and Solutions

Unintended exposure of ports can invite unauthorized access and potential breaches. Review your firewall rules and ensure appropriate ingress and egress restrictions:

```
# Limit access to container ports from specific IPs or subnets
$ iptables -A INPUT -p tcp --dport <port_number> -s <ip_range> -j
    ACCEPT
```

146

Establish rules to whitelist known IP addresses and deny all unnecessary traffic.

- Tackling Latency and Performance Bottlenecks

Network latency or degraded performance can arise from improper load balancing, excessive resource consumption, or network congestion.

- Load Balancing and Resource Management

Ensure load balancers distribute traffic evenly across containers, preventing overload. Use tools like HAProxy or NGINX load balancers in front of applications to direct traffic efficiently.

Implement resource limits and requests to prevent network congestion:

```
$ podman run --memory=512m --cpus=1.0 <container_image>
```

Specify limits to ensure containers do not overwhelm available network bandwidth, maintaining performance stability.

- Utilizing Logging and Monitoring Tools

Effective troubleshooting relies heavily on both real-time monitoring and historical log analysis. Leverage logging frameworks and monitoring solutions to detect anomalies, track usage patterns, and capture detailed diagnostics.

- Log Inspection and Usage

Container logs reveal insights into internal networking issues and potential failures:

```
$ podman logs <container_id>
```

Review logs for indications of timeout, DNS errors, or connection refusals, helping identify failure points.

- Advanced Diagnosis with Network Analysis Tools

For persistent or complex issues, network analysis tools can offer more detailed inspection. Utilize utilities like `tcpdump` or `wireshark` within the container environment to capture and analyze packet transmissions.

```
$ podman exec -it <container_name> tcpdump -i eth0
```

Capture live packet data for deep inspection, revealing traffic patterns and anomalies that might contribute to disconnects or performance issues.

- Integrated Troubleshooting with Orchestrators

In orchestrated environments like those managed by Kubernetes, issues may stem not only from individual containers but the broader infrastructure. Employ orchestrator-specific troubleshooting techniques, examining pod logs, event histories, and network policies.

```
$ kubectl describe pod <pod_name>
$ kubectl logs <pod_name>
```

Use these commands to explore possible misconfigurations at the orchestration layer, ensuring the root cause is promptly addressed.

Chapter 6

Persistent Storage in Podman

This chapter explores persistent storage solutions in Podman, focusing on volumes and bind mounts, and their roles in data preservation. It offers comprehensive guidance on creating and managing volumes to ensure data continuity across container restarts. Best practices for data management within containers are discussed to maintain integrity and availability. Additionally, it addresses security measures to protect stored data, emphasizing strategies to mitigate risks and ensure secure access within containerized environments, thereby providing a stable infrastructure for application data.

6.1. Understanding Container Storage Concepts

Container storage is a critical aspect of modern application deployment due to the ephemeral nature of containers. Persistent storage pioneered solutions that ensure data is retained even when containers are deleted or recreated. Understanding these storage concepts is essential for efficient data management within containerized environments, particularly in Podman. This section discusses persistent storage, its significance, and various storage technologies that integrate with containers, focusing on Podman.

Persistent storage's primary role is to maintain data beyond the lifecycle of a container instance. Unlike traditional application storage, where data persists directly on the infrastructure, containers pose challenges due to their transient state. As containers facilitate componentized applications—each running independently and potentially on different nodes—the need for a consistent storage layer becomes paramount. Persistent storage satisfies this need by enabling stateful applications to maintain continuity, especially crucial for databases, message brokers, and applications requiring immutability.

Podman, an open-source container management engine, provides tools for managing container storage efficiently. One fundamental concept within Podman is the separation of storage from the container's lifecycle. This separation is achieved through volumes and bind mounts, both integral to Podman's storage system, and they offer different capabilities and use cases suitable for a variety of operational requirements.

Volumes in Podman represent an independent storage abstraction that persists beyond container termination. They are managed by the Podman engine and can be easily shared across multiple containers. This level of abstraction is beneficial in scenarios requiring decoupled storage from the filesystem, which simplifies data migration and backup processes.

Here is a simple demonstration of creating a volume in Podman using the command line:

```
podman volume create my_volume
```

The command above initializes a volume named `my_volume`, which Podman handles independently, providing clean storage management. This volume can then be mounted into one or multiple containers, offering a convenient approach to persistent shared storage.

In contrast, bind mounts provide a direct link between the host filesystem and container's filesystem. Bind mounts offer exact control over storage paths and granularity, proving useful in development environments where source code on the host must be accessible inside a container for rapid iteration and debugging.

The command below illustrates a bind mount setup with Podman:

```
podman run -v /host_path:/container_path my_image
```

This command mounts the host directory `/host_path` into the container's `/container_path` directory, offering direct access to host data.

Another essential consideration within container storage concepts is the underlying storage drivers that Podman employs, which interact with the host filesystem, enabling the abstraction and manipulation of container filesystem layers. Storage drivers are responsible for implementing the layered storage architecture, allowing Podman containers to use filesystems like OverlayFS, Btrfs, or ZFS.

OverlayFS, frequently used in Podman, provides a layered mechanism for images and containers. It consolidates different layers into a single unified image, optimizing storage usage by reducing duplicate data. In practice, this means modifications to files within a container don't alter the original image files; instead, changes are written to an upper

151

layer. Understanding this layering concept is crucial for effectively diagnosing and troubleshooting storage-related issues in containerized
environments.

Here's a practical way storage drivers interact in Podman's architecture:

```
podman info --format "{{.Store.GraphDriverName}}"
```

Executing the above command provides the current storage driver used
by Podman, facilitating administrators in tailoring storage strategies
according to their performance and scalability requirements.

Recognizing storage as a pivotal component of container platforms directs emphasis towards container orchestration systems like Kubernetes, which embed advanced storage capabilities. Kubernetes integrates with container runtimes like Podman and endorses persistent
storage solutions, termed Persistent Volumes (PVs), which bind storage in a manner abstracted from particular infrastructure, supporting
diverse storage backends and scaling data storage requirements ro-
bustly.

To provision storage across Kubernetes clusters using Podman, Persistent Volumes (PVs) and Persistent Volume Claims (PVCs) stand central to Kubernetes' storage provision. PVs define the actual storage options, external to the Pods, meanwhile, PVCs are requests by users to
access specific capacities and types of storage.

Illustrating a Kubernetes PV definition:

```
apiVersion: v1
kind: PersistentVolume
metadata:
  name: my-pv
spec:
  capacity:
    storage: 10Gi
  accessModes:
    - ReadWriteOnce
```

```
persistentVolumeReclaimPolicy: Retain
...
```

Persistent Volumes, such as my-pv outlined above, allow specifying capacity, access modes, and reclamation policies, essential for ensuring appropriate access control and lifecycle management of storage resources.

Connecting into the more traditional domain, understanding Network Attached Storage (NAS) and its integrated use for containers stands notable. NAS solutions provide a centralized data store accessible over a network, often supporting high performance and significant scalability. Within container environments, NAS can serve as a backing store for volumes, offering a united and persistent storage layer capable of spanning multiple hosts, fostering enhanced operational resilience and redundancy strategies.

Furthermore, Storage Area Networks (SAN) serve as another robust enterprise storage solution. SAN offers a high-performance interconnection between storage devices and servers, augmenting container storage capabilities, especially when high throughput and low latency are demanded by applications relying on substantial synchronous data read and write operations.

In the broader context of cloud-native environments, container storage solutions advance toward dynamic, API-driven storages—such as the Container Storage Interface (CSI)—that decouple storage provisioning, permitting vendors to provide pluggable storage solutions integrated seamlessly with container orchestration frameworks. CSI is an emerging standard, accelerating storage provider involvement across cloud ecosystems and driving innovations in persistent storage technologies.

Moreover, recent enhancements in storage technologies for containers exhibit expanded use cases through edge computing. Edge environments pose unique challenges requiring low latency, high reliability storage options, which translate into specialized techniques to handle persistent storage efficiently at the edge where conventional approaches become insufficient.

An understanding of these advanced storage options and concepts sets forth a solid foundation for managing data in containerized environments using Podman. As technologies evolve and newer paradigms of container storage emerge, staying abreast of these innovations enables deploying, monitoring, and maintaining sophisticated container-based applications with enhanced efficacy and resilience.

6.2. Volumes vs. Bind Mounts

In containerized environments, encapsulating software and its dependencies within containers introduces challenges related to persistent storage. Unlike traditional systems, where applications are tethered to physical or virtual machines with direct filesystem access, containers are ephemeral by design. This ephemeral nature means any data stored within a container is lost when the container is removed. To overcome this, container management systems provide mechanisms such as volumes and bind mounts to persist data, enabling containers to interact effectively with the host filesystem. This section delves into a comprehensive comparison between volumes and bind mounts within Podman, outlining their distinct characteristics, use-cases, and implementation strategies.

Volumes and bind mounts, though conceptually similar in that they both map storage resources from the host to the container, serve different purposes and operate under unique paradigms within Podman. Understanding these differences is crucial to selecting the optimal data persistence approach tailored to various application requirements.

Volumes in the context of Podman are a native storage abstraction that is independent of the underlying host filesystem. Managed by Podman, volumes can be thought of as a high-level construct that Podman utilizes to maintain data that persists regardless of the container's lifecycle. One of the primary advantages of volumes is their abstraction; they offer a managed solution that is isolated from the host operating environment, ensuring portability and easy backups.

Creation of a volume in Podman is straightforward, as illustrated below:

```
podman volume create data_volume
```

This command creates a volume called "data_volume". Once a volume is established, it can be attached to containers at runtime, providing persistent storage without explicit host path interference:

```
podman run -d --name app --mount type=volume,source=data_volume,
    target=/app/data httpd
```

Here, the "data_volume" is attached to the running container, facilitating persistent data storage at location /app/data within the container.

Volumes offer several advantages, particularly for stateful applications that require consistent storage interaction. Because volumes are decoupled from host file structures, they provide an ideal solution for sharing data between containers without exposing underlying host directories. This level of encapsulation supports seamless migration of applications across various environments (dev, test, prod) with minimal configuration adjustments.

Volumes' limitations arise in certain development scenarios requiring enhanced visibility into a container's filesystem. For instance, during debugging or rapid application-specific configurations, volumes might obscure the underlying file dynamics, requiring alternative solutions like bind mounts for more integrated development workflows.

Conversely, bind mounts provide a direct linkage between a host direc-

155

tory or file and a container's filesystem. Unlike volumes, bind mounts map specific directories from the host directly into the container, enabling the container to access or modify the exact data files stored on the host. This direct access can be instrumental in scenarios necessitating fine-grained control over the file paths or when distinct host systems share data through standardized directory structures.

Setting up a bind mount is accomplished with Podman as follows:

```
podman run -d --name webapp -v /host/data:/app/data nginx
```

The command above mounts the host directory /host/data to /app/data within the container, granting direct access to and from the container.

Bind mounts excel in development environments where modifications on the host should immediately reflect in the container, promoting agile development and testing practices. For example, web developers leveraging bind mounts can edit source files on the host and instantly see changes in a running containerized web server without restarting the container.

However, bind mounts come with their own complexities and potential pitfalls. The tight coupling between container storage and host filesystem paths implies that misconfigurations or errors can have ripple effects outside the container, affecting host system integrity. Additionally, bind mounts' dependency on absolute paths makes configuration across different environments cumbersome, affecting portability and leading to increased complexity in environments requiring standardized directory hierarchies.

To evaluate the trade-offs, consider an example scenario involving a continuous integration (CI) pipeline processing vast datasets. The choice between volumes and bind mounts can significantly impact performance, security, and maintainability. Using bind mounts may be advantageous where datasets are frequently updated from external sources stored on the host, optimizing access speeds. Conversely, using volumes could enhance data consistency across build stages, allowing seamless sharing and maintenance of preconfigured data states without host dependency.

In containerized database management, choosing between volumes and bind mounts involves carefully weighing data security, performance, and portability requirements. While volumes offer a level of abstraction that may be advantageous for encrypted data storage, reducing the risk of unauthorized host access, bind mounts may yield performance improvements in scenarios demanding high-speed data transactions directly between the database and host storage devices.

Analyzing emerging patterns in cloud-native applications, volumes align with modern infrastructure trends towards decoupling services from hardware specifics, supporting microservices architectures where service isolation and independent scalability are prioritized. Conversely, bind mounts fit legacy systems or transitional environments where adherence to established directory frameworks and file sharing is necessary to complement existing application architectures.

Finally, advancements in storage plugins and container orchestration platforms bolster the use of volumes through enhanced features such as dynamic provisioning, automated scaling, and integration with storage backends supporting distributed storage, like Ceph or GlusterFS, making volumes an increasingly attractive option for high-availability and high-redundancy requirements in multi-node deployments.

In sum, both volumes and bind mounts serve critical roles in achieving persistent storage in containerized environments. Their respective advantages and limitations make clear that selection depends on the specific use case requirements, the environment's architectural considerations, and the actual development and operational needs. The nuanced understanding of these traits enables strategic decisions, capturing the benefits of containers' flexibility while ensuring robust, persistent data handling in complex deployment ecosystems.

6.3. Creating and Managing Volumes

Volumes represent a pivotal concept in containerized environments, facilitating data persistence beyond the ephemeral lifecycle of container instances. Managing volumes efficiently within Podman requires an understanding of their creation, utilization, and lifecycle management to ensure optimal use in varied deployment scenarios. This section elucidates these processes while providing deep insights into strategies and considerations for effective volume management.

Volumes in Podman serve as independent managed storage entities abstracted from host file systems, providing the advantage of decoupling persistent storage from the specific container environment. They are particularly useful for ensuring data continuity across container restarts and enabling multi-container data sharing.

The process of creating a volume in Podman is intuitive, requiring a single command:

```
podman volume create app_data
```

This command initializes a new volume named app_data. By default, Podman names volumes with unique identifiers for easy identification and management across environments. The naming convention is crucial, particularly in environments with complex multi-service architectures, where improper naming could lead to confusion or unintentional data overwrites.

Once created, volumes can be seamlessly integrated into containers using the volume mount option, facilitating controlled access to persistent storage:

```
podman run -d --name web_service -v app_data:/var/www/html nginx
```

In this example, the app_data volume is mounted at /var/www/html inside the web_service container. Such configurations are instrumental in scenarios requiring the storage of application state or assets—such as user uploads or generated reports—ensuring that data remains intact regardless of the container being stopped or removed.

Volumes in Podman extend their utility by supporting additional configuration parameters during setup. An advanced feature includes driver options that customize storage characteristics to align with specific performance or redundancy requirements. These options cater to diverse storage backends, enabling administrators to tailor volumes according to organizational policy or workload demands.

Critical considerations arise in the lifecycle management of volumes, encompassing tasks such as audits, updates, and deprecation of deprecated or orphaned volumes. Best practices suggest regularly listing available volumes to maintain a clear overview of active and inactive resources:

```
podman volume ls
```

Identifying volumes no longer in use is fundamental to efficient resource utilization and maintaining a clean operating environment. It ensures residual data does not occupy valuable storage space or inadvertently expose sensitive information. Following identification, volumes can be prudently removed using:

```
podman volume rm unused_volume
```

This operation demands caution, as it results in irrevocable data deletion. Implementing robust volume-naming policies assists in avoiding inadvertent deletions, emphasizing the significance of thorough documentation and collaborative oversight in large teams.

For environments demanding advanced storage resilience and redundancy, Podman permits integration with external storage solutions, such as distributed filesystems (e.g., Ceph, GlusterFS). Such configurations enable volumes to extend their capabilities beyond a single host, offering scalability and fault tolerance essential in high-availability deployments.

The following represents a conceptual integration snippet with distributed storage, assuming a backend configuration exists:

```
podman volume create --driver glusterfs --opt device=10.10.10.10:/
    myvol app_shared_data
```

This command binds the GlusterFS volume `myvol` at IP address `10.10.10.10` to the Podman volume `app_shared_data`, permitting cross-container node access and sharing, integral in clustered service architectures.

Security in volume management becomes increasingly paramount, particularly when dealing with sensitive or critical data. Podman supports mechanisms for credential management and access restrictions (e.g., SELinux policies), safeguarding data from unwarranted access or manipulation by unauthorized containers. Such measures align with enterprise-grade security protocols, ensuring data confidentiality and integrity across container workflows.

Enforcement of such policies, as shown here with SELinux:

```
podman run -d --name secure_app -v app_data:/sensitive_data:Z
    my_secure_image
```

The :Z option relabels the bind target with an SELinux label, equipping the volume with stringent access controls in line with the container's security context.

Additionally, monitoring volume usage trends over time helps predict future storage needs and optimize resource allocation. Implementing automated monitoring and alerting systems for volume capacity near-thresholds is a recommended strategy for maintaining uninterrupted service performance, aligning storage provisioning with real-time demand.

Considerations for backups and data recovery remain a cornerstone of volume management strategy. Regular backups encapsulate volume contents, preserving application states, and reducing the impact of accidental data loss or corruption. Various tools and practices exist for orchestrating snapshot-based backups or integrating with enterprise-grade storage solutions offering automated backup services, an essential aspect for business continuity planning.

An example of a simple local backup process using Podman:

```
podman run --rm --volumes-from app_container -v $(pwd):/backup
    busybox tar czvf /backup/app_data.tar.gz /var/www/html
```

Here, the container's data directory is archived to the host's current working directory, manifesting a straightforward method for volume data checkpointing. As environments scale, more sophisticated tools would replace such manual interventions, optimizing data protection across storage systems.

In advanced use cases, dynamic volume provisioning capabilities empower developers to automate storage configuration as part of the application deployment lifecycle. This automation facilitates DevOps practices through infrastructure as code, reducing onboarding friction and ensuring storage specifications are embedded within declarative deployment templates.

Finally, as organizations continue evolving their IT landscapes towards cloud-native ecosystems, the trend towards adopting Container Storage Interface (CSI)-compliant storage management extends Podman's volume management capabilities. This advancement promises a greater variety of network-attached and cloud-based storage integrations, expanding Podman's adaptability and enterprise throughput potential.

The strategic deployment and consistent management of volumes within Podman not only enhance data longevity and service resilience but also enhance the overall robustness and flexibility of containerized applications transitioning into production at scale.

6.4. Using Persistent Storage in Containers

The use of persistent storage in containers addresses one of the fundamental challenges of containerized environments—their inherent statelessness. Containers are designed as ephemeral entities; they start, run various processes, and upon exit, leave no trace behind. This design paradigm optimizes for speed, scalability, and resource efficiency, but poses a significant challenge for applications requiring data persistence across container restarts and failures. This section examines the methodologies and strategies for deploying persistent storage solutions in containers using Podman, emphasizing practical implementation and informed decision-making.

At the core of employing persistent storage is understanding the types of data that need persistence. Applications generally fall into two categories: stateless and stateful. Stateless applications, like frontend web servers, don't rely on any ongoing state between requests, while stateful applications, such as databases, inherently require persistent storage solutions to maintain their data integrity.

In Podman, persistent storage can be implemented using volumes or bind mounts, both of which introduce a stable storage interface independent of the container lifecycle. Volumes provide a means to decouple application data from individual container instances, fostering portability and replication. A practical example of employing a volume to enforce persistent storage is as follows:

```
podman run -d --name persistent_app -v app_volume:/mnt/data my_image
```

In this configuration, 'app_volume' ensures any data written to '/mnt/data' within the 'persistent_app' container persists beyond the container's shutdown or failure. This approach is central to applications with consistent states or those performing cumulative updates to data over time, such as logging services or transactional systems.

Layering additional security and performance enhancements on persistent storage involves configuring the underlying storage backend used by Podman. Storage solutions such as OverlayFS, Btrfs, or ZFS provide different features related to performance, snapshots, and data integrity. For instance, Btrfs allows for easy data snapshotting and rollback, enhancing application resilience and providing a comprehensive history of data states that can be restored as required:

```
podman info --format "{{.Store.GraphDriver}}"
```

The command above queries Podman for the current storage driver, allowing administrators to optimize persistent storage model configurations according to specific performance needs or operational policy frameworks.

Applications integrating persistent storage often extend into orchestrated environments using Kubernetes. Persistent storage is managed in Kubernetes using Persistent Volumes (PVs) and Persistent Volume Claims (PVCs). Kubernetes handles the automation of these storage resources, enabling more sophisticated provisioning dynamically, responsive to application demand.

A typical Persistent Volume configuration in Kubernetes integrated with Podman might look like this:

```
apiVersion: v1
kind: PersistentVolume
```

```
metadata:
  name: shared-storage
spec:
  capacity:
    storage: 100Gi
  accessModes:
    - ReadWriteMany
  persistentVolumeReclaimPolicy: Retain
  ...
```

The configuration above initializes a PV with 'ReadWriteMany' access, allowing simultaneous read and write connections from multiple pods, thereby supporting collaborative applications or clustered databases.

Another essential consideration when utilizing persistent storage is data backup and recovery. In environments relying heavily on containerized workloads, data snapshots and backups constitute vital components of maintaining data integrity and ensuring rapid recovery from incidents. Implementing a robust backup solution involves creating regular copies of volume data, leveraging tools that interact with Podman's storage mechanisms:

```
podman run --rm --volumes-from my_app -v $(pwd):/backup busybox tar
    czvf /backup/app_backup.tar.gz /mnt/data
```

The above command facilitates the creation of a backup 'app_backup.tar.gz' from data located at '/mnt/data', emphasizing an approach that utilizes Podman-managed volumes.

In practical deployment scenarios, using CI/CD pipelines and automation tools significantly enhances the orchestration of persistent storage management. Automation scripts and configuration management tools, such as Ansible or Terraform, ensure consistent volume provisioning and data integrity, reducing manual intervention in scaling or recovery operations.

For applications requiring persistent data encryption, Podman supports extending secure storage configurations that include volume-

164

level encryption. Encrypting data at rest mitigates risks from unauthorized access to raw storage devices, satisfying compliance with regulatory requirements and industry best practices:

```
podman run -d --name encrypted_app -v secrets_volume:/secure_data:ro,
    z my_encrypted_image
```

The use of the ':ro,z' option illustrates the configuration of read-only access with SELinux labeling to bolster security. Advanced implementation might include interfacing with external systems for encryption key management, optimizing volume security without sacrificing usability or access speed.

Persistent storage also facilitates container workloads that span across distributed or hybrid cloud environments. Solutions like Ceph, Amazon EBS, or Azure Files provide network-attached storage that scales transparently, supporting a wide range of workloads without geographical constraints, making them well-suited for distributed applications that rely on consistent data availability.

As container technology continues to integrate more deeply within enterprise infrastructure, understanding persistent storage strategies and principles becomes increasingly essential. Emerging trends in edge computing place additional demands on storage systems, further pushing the boundaries of traditional container and storage interactions.

Ultimately, persistent storage within Podman, executed with a careful balance of performance, security, and scalability considerations, enhances the overall reliability and robustness of containerized applications. Whether through native volumes, external storage integrations, or automated data management strategies, mastering the use of persistent storage is integral to leveraging the full potential of modern containerized environments, ensuring data remains consistently available across dynamic and scalable deployments.

6.5. Best Practices for Data Management

Effective data management within containerized environments is critical to maintaining data integrity, ensuring availability, and optimizing performance. As organizations increasingly adopt container technologies like Podman to deploy and scale applications, understanding and implementing data management best practices become pivotal. This section delves into key strategies and methodologies to efficiently manage data in containerized ecosystems.

A foundational principle of data management in containers is the clear delineation between ephemeral and persistent data. Applications benefit from this distinction by isolating transient operational data—such as compute-intensive logs—from persistent data requiring longevity. This approach enhances storage organization, minimizes unnecessary data retention, and optimizes backup strategies. Containers fostering this separation are easier to scale and manage, reducing storage overhead and potential data loss.

The choice between volumes and bind mounts, inherent to Podman, should be guided by specific use case requirements. As a general best practice, volumes are recommended for managing persistent data due to their abstraction, portability, and ease of use across diverse environments. Their managed nature simplifies backups and migrations:

```
podman volume create persistent_volume
podman run --name app --mount type=volume,src=persistent_volume,
    target=/app/data my_container
```

Here, `persistent_volume` maintains critical application data outside the container, reinforcing data continuity and reuse.

Embracing automation through Infrastructure as Code (IaC) is crucial for consistent data management. Tools like Ansible, Terraform, and Kubernetes configurations serve as blueprints for provisioning and managing storage resources systematically. This ensures repeatability, reduces human errors, and accelerates environment recovery after failures.

Snapshot technologies can enhance data availability and disaster recovery efforts. Implementing snapshot-based backup strategies, enabled with tools supporting Btrfs or ZFS backends, provides incremental backups, easing daily operations and reducing recovery time objectives (RTO):

```
btrfs subvolume snapshot /mnt/data /mnt/snapshots/backup-$(date +%F)
```

This approach captures real-time application states, proving essential in rollback scenarios following erroneous changes or corrupted data entries.

Data security cannot be overemphasized, particularly in environments housing sensitive or regulated information. Adopting encryption both in transit and at rest ensures data confidentiality. Volume encryption mechanisms and secure access protocols must be standard practice:

```
podman run --name secure_app -v my_encrypted_volume:/secure_data:ro,z
    my_secure_image
```

Advanced implementations could incorporate orchestrated key management solutions to streamline encryption without complicating access processes.

Data governance policies define the frameworks for data handling, consent, and auditing. Establishing precise data classification policies clarifies storage requirements and guides the segmentation of sensitive information. Enforcing clear access control mechanisms aligns with privacy regulations and organizational security standards, restricting unauthorized container and host interactions.

Monitoring and analytics in containerized environments bolster data management by capturing usage metrics, patterns, and performance insights. Real-time monitoring tools alert anomalies in data access patterns, indicating potential security breaches or operational inefficiencies:

```
podman stats --all
```

This command aids in monitoring resource usage metrics, informing administrators of ongoing performance or storage anomalies within the containers.

Data locality strategies optimize performance by strategically placing data closer to compute resources. This consideration is especially vital in cloud-native architectures where data-resident services reduce latency and enhance application responsiveness.

In cloud and hybrid cloud deployments, leveraging managed storage services (e.g., AWS EBS, Azure Managed Disks) provides scalable and reliable storage options. These services natively support dynamic provisioning and integration with container orchestration platforms, thus aligning with best practices for elasticity and fault-tolerant infrastructures.

Edge computing introduces unique challenges due to decentralized architectures. Efficient data management at the edge necessitates lightweight, low footprint storage solutions that synchronize with central data repositories. Container-native edge solutions integrated with robust synchronization mechanisms support consistency across distributed nodes.

Continuously evolving best practices denote a need for adopting emerging technologies, tools, and frameworks. Keeping abreast of the latest updates in storage solutions, security standards, and container management systems ensures ongoing alignment with industry trends and standards, empowering organizations to maintain competitive effectiveness and reliability.

Mastering efficient data management within containers leverages the inherent strengths of containerization while minimizing the attendant weaknesses. By adopting methodical practices concerning storage isolation, automation, security, and governance, and through engagement with modern tools and platforms, organizations harness the full potential of container technology for consistent, robust, and scalable application environments.

6.6. Securing Storage for Containers

In a world increasingly reliant on containerized environments, the importance of securing storage cannot be overstated. Containers, by their very nature, introduce unique security challenges linked to their orchestration, isolation, and the ephemeral nature of their operations. As such, securing data storage for these containers is critical to ensuring data integrity, preventing unauthorized access, and mitigating potential breaches. This section presents an in-depth exploration of the strategies, techniques, and considerations essential for fortifying storage security within Podman-managed container deployments.

- **Storage Isolation and Access Control:** The cornerstone of securing storage in containers is the principle of isolation. Containers should operate in an environment where data access is rigorously controlled, ensuring each container has access only to the data it needs. This access control limits the blast radius of potential breaches.

  Volumes in Podman can be secured by restricting them to specific access modes. For example, implementing read-only volumes ensures that containers can read but cannot modify sensitive data:

```
podman run --name readonly_app -v secure_volume:/app/data:
ro nginx
```

Using the ':ro' flag, the 'secure_volume' is mounted in a read-only mode, thereby defending against accidental or malicious data alterations.

Another layer of protection involves utilizing cgroups and namespaces to enforce isolation at the kernel level. These mechanisms allow you to segregate processes, file systems, and resource limits, ensuring that even if a container is compromised, access to other system components and data is minimized.

- **Encryption: In-Transit and At-Rest:** Encrypting data is a critical security measure that protects against unauthorized access. Data should be encrypted both when at rest—i.e., stored on a disk—and in transit—i.e., during communication between containers and external systems.

For data at rest, Podman supports the integration of Linux Unified Key Setup (LUKS) encrypted volumes. This provides robust encryption to secure data on storage devices:

```
# Example command to set up LUKS encryption
cryptsetup luksFormat /dev/sdX
cryptsetup luksOpen /dev/sdX luksencrypted
mkfs.ext4 /dev/mapper/luksencrypted
mount /dev/mapper/luksencrypted /secure_mount
podman run --name encrypted_data_app -v /secure_mount:/app/
data nginx
```

Data in transit should be secured using protocols such as TLS (Transport Layer Security). Ensuring all internal and external container communications are encrypted prevents eavesdropping and man-in-the-middle attacks:

```
podman run -d --name tls_app -v /certs:/etc/certs:ro -e "
SSL_CERT=/etc/certs/server.pem" my_tls_image
```

By mounting certificates and enforcing their use within the application, the communication can be kept secure.

- **Implementing Layered Security Policies:** Security best practices promote a layered approach, often known as defense in depth. Establish redundancy in security measures so that, if one layer fails, others continue to protect the storage data.

  Podman can be configured to enforce SELinux (Security-Enhanced Linux) policies that govern container access to storage:

  ```
  podman run --name secure_selinux_app -v volumelabel:/data:Z
      my_secure_image
  ```

  The ':Z' and ':z' options adjust the SELinux context for the volume, thereby ensuring containers adhere to stringent access controls defined within SELinux policy frameworks.

- **Regular Audits and Monitoring:** Implementing monitoring and regular audits ensures storage systems remain secure over time. Tools such as Grafana, Prometheus, or ELK Stack can provide insights into access patterns, modified configurations, and anomalous behaviors.

  Additionally, enabling audit logs for container operations can help track unauthorized access attempts and data breaches:

  ```
  podman logs secure_app_container
  ```

  Audit systems should continuously verify that containers adhere to the organization's security policies, alerting administrators to discrepancies and potential breaches in real-time.

- **Integrating with Key Management Services:** Effective management of encryption keys is essential for maintaining a secure storage system. Key Management Services (KMS) offer cen-

tralized control over data keys, enhancing security and simplifying operations, such as revoking compromised keys or rotating
old keys:

For example, within AWS:

```
aws kms encrypt --key-id alias/my-key --plaintext fileb://
   mydata --output text --query CiphertextBlob
```

Using a KMS improves the robustness of cryptographic operations, reduces reliance on local hardcoded keys, and provides logging and auditing features to track usage patterns.

- **Secure Configuration Management:** Containers should always be deployed from minimal, secure base images, reducing
  the attack surface. Podman security scans, such as Podman's native image scanning capabilities, help ensure containers are free
  from vulnerabilities:

```
podman image trust set --type=reject default
podman scan myimage
```

Security scanning practices ensure that only signed, trusted images are deployed, protecting against the introduction of insecure
dependencies.

- **Distributed Storage and Network Security:** For
  distributed applications utilizing Network Attached Storage
  (NAS) or distributed file systems, network security becomes
  integral to storage protection. This involves securing the
  communication channels between distributed storage nodes
  and container hosts:

```
podman network create --driver bridge secure_bridge
podman run --network secure_bridge -d --name secure_net_app
   nginx
```

Utilizing secure, isolated network configurations for container communication supports data security by further constraining potential attack vectors.

Securing container storage is an ongoing endeavor that must evolve alongside the dynamic landscape of threats and technologies. By integrating best practices such as rigorous isolation, robust encryption, diligent monitoring, and utilizing cutting-edge security solutions, organizations can effectively mitigate risks and protect their valuable data assets. As container management systems like Podman continue to advance, maintaining vigilance and adaptability remains essential to upholding data security in complex and distributed environments.

Chapter 7

Advanced Podman Commands and Operations

This chapter delves into advanced functionalities of Podman, highlighting automated scripts for container operations and the benefits of rootless mode. It discusses implementing health checks and monitoring containers to maintain operational health. Resource management strategies are covered to optimize container performance. The concept of pods for managing multi-container applications is explored, along with the integration of Podman with systemd for treating containers as system services. These advanced operations enhance users' ability to efficiently manage complex container scenarios, ensuring robust and scalable environments.

7.1. Leveraging Podman for Scripted Automation

In scripting environments where container automation is essential, Podman provides a powerful set of tools that can be seamlessly integrated into scripts to manage container operations efficiently. This section explores the practical application of using Podman in scripted automation, emphasizing how to leverage its comprehensive suite of commands to automate various tasks related to container management. The focus will be on understanding the scripting capabilities of Podman, highlighting key commands, scripting considerations, and presenting illustrative examples that demonstrate its application in real-world scenarios.

Podman provides a command-line interface compatible with Docker, thereby making it straightforward for users familiar with Docker to transition to Podman. This compatibility extends to many commands and operations, allowing for a minimal learning curve for users transitioning their automated systems to Podman. However, Podman introduces unique features that enhance its use in scripting scenarios.

Advantages of using Podman for scripted automation include its rootless operation, enhanced security features, the concept of pods, and ease of integration with Linux tools and scripting languages. Bypassing the requirement for a daemon, Podman eliminates a potential single point of failure, enhancing reliability in production environments.

```
#!/bin/bash

# Variables
IMAGE="nginx:latest"
CONTAINER_NAME="my_nginx"

# Pull the latest image
podman pull $IMAGE

# Check if the container is already running, then stop and remove it
if podman ps -a --format="{{.Names}}" | grep -Eq "^${CONTAINER_NAME}$
    "; then
```

```
  podman stop $CONTAINER_NAME
  podman rm $CONTAINER_NAME
fi

# Run a new container
podman run -d --name $CONTAINER_NAME -p 8080:80 $IMAGE

# Verify the container is running
if podman ps --format "{{.Names}}" | grep -q "${CONTAINER_NAME}";
    then
  echo "Container $CONTAINER_NAME is running."
else
  echo "Failed to start container $CONTAINER_NAME."
fi
```

In this example, a Bash script leverages Podman commands to perform a basic operation—pulling an image, removing any existing container with the specified name, and starting a new container with that image. Such scripts are foundational for automated deployment strategies, allowing users to dynamically manage resources with little manual intervention.

- Script Execution and Output Management

When executing scripts with Podman commands, handling outputs is crucial for ensuring that the automation performs as expected and that errors are promptly addressed. Redirecting outputs to logs is a common practice, especially in environments where audit trails are necessary. This can be accomplished using simple redirections in shell scripts:

```
#!/bin/bash

LOG_FILE="podman_operations.log"

# Redirect stdout to LOG_FILE
exec 1>>$LOG_FILE

# Pull an image and output to log
echo "Pulling the latest nginx image..."
podman pull nginx:latest
```

177

```
echo "Checking running containers..."
podman ps

exec 1>&-
```

During the script execution, all output of commands is appended to the podman_operations.log file, ensuring that logs are kept for review and analysis. This approach helps maintain operational transparency and can assist in debugging or in meeting compliance requirements.

- Scheduling Automated Scripts

Automation scripts can be scheduled to execute at regular intervals using cron jobs on Linux systems. This allows administrators to automate repetitive tasks such as container updates, backups, and monitoring.

To schedule the above script with cron, use the following steps:

- Open the cron editor by typing crontab -e.

- Add a new entry for the script. For example, to run the script daily at midnight:

```
0 0 * * * /path/to/podman_script.sh
```

This cron entry ensures that the script executes every day at midnight, pulling the latest image and ensuring the specified container is running as expected.

- Configuration Management and Environment Variables

Podman automation scripts often rely on environment variables for configuration management. This practice increases the scripts' flexibility, allowing operations across different environments (development, testing, production) to be performed with minimal changes. The following example demonstrates how to use environment variables within a Podman automation script:

```bash
#!/bin/bash

# Set environment variables
export IMAGE_NAME="nginx:latest"
export CONTAINER_PORT=8080
export HOST_PORT=80

# Pull the specified image
podman pull $IMAGE_NAME

# Run a container using environment variables
podman run -d -p $HOST_PORT:$CONTAINER_PORT $IMAGE_NAME
```

This script uses environment variables to determine the image name and port mappings, facilitating easy alternation between various configurations by simply changing the environment variable values without needing to directly modify the script.

- Integrating Podman with Popular Scripting Languages

While Bash scripts are ubiquitous for automating tasks with Podman, integrating Podman commands with higher-level programming languages such as Python can provide additional flexibility, functionality, and robustness. Libraries such as subprocess in Python allow execution of Podman commands, enabling complex decision-making and handling based on command outputs.

Here is an example of using Python to automate Podman:

```python
import subprocess

def execute_command(command):
    result = subprocess.run(command, shell=True, capture_output=True,
      text=True)
    return result.stdout, result.stderr
```

```
image = "nginx:latest"
container_name = "nginx_server"

# Pull image
out, err = execute_command(f"podman pull {image}")

# Check if the container exists, stop and remove it
out, err = execute_command(f"podman ps -a --format='{{{{.Names}}}}'")
if container_name in out:
    execute_command(f"podman stop {container_name}")
    execute_command(f"podman rm {container_name}")

# Run a new container
execute_command(f"podman run -d --name {container_name} -p 8080:80 {
    image}")
```

This example demonstrates integrating Podman with Python, allowing for more complex logic than what is typically done with shell scripts. The subprocess module captures outputs and errors, facilitating richer error handling and debugging activities.

- Enhanced Security Practices in Scripted Automation

Automation also necessitates stringent security practices. Since Podman can operate in rootless mode, it is inherently more secure, providing a level of isolation that reduces the risk commonly associated with running containers as root. Additionally, storing sensitive data such as credentials or tokens securely is essential. Avoid hardcoding these values directly in scripts; use environment variables or secret management services wherever possible to inject them securely at runtime.

Within a Podman context, implementing Secure Shell (SSH) and encryption protocols are also advisable for remote management and operation, keeping communication between systems secure. Moreover, adhere to the principle of least privilege by only granting necessary permissions to scripts and user accounts used for automation.

Podman's ability to integrate well with traditional and modern scripting techniques makes it a powerful tool for container automation. Its focus on security, both from its rootless architecture and flexible configuration options, positions it as an excellent choice for organizations seeking reliable and automatable container solutions. Whether for simple automated tasks or complex multi-step workflows, Podman's comprehensive command suite and scripting capabilities provide all the necessary tools to achieve high levels of automation efficiency and effectiveness.

7.2. Using Podman in Rootless Mode

Podman distinguishes itself from other container management systems with a significant feature: the ability to run containers in rootless mode. This capability enhances security by minimizing the risks associated with running processes as the root user. Rootless mode enables users to initiate containers without requiring increased system-level privileges, effectively segregating container operations from potential host vulnerabilities. This attribute is critical in environments where security policies mandate strict access control and restrictions over system operations.

Rootless mode achieves its functionality through user namespaces, a feature in the Linux kernel that re-maps user IDs (UIDs) and group IDs (GIDs) for processes. This mechanism allows containers to be executed as if they are running as root within their namespace, while actually being executed with non-root privileges on the host system.

- **Setting Up Podman for Rootless Operation**

Before utilizing rootless mode, it is essential to ensure that the user environment is appropriately configured. Rootless containers leverage the user's existing environment, requiring specific configurations to operate efficiently.

Firstly, verify whether rootless mode is already configured:

```
podman info --format '{{.host.Security}}'
```

This command outputs the security settings of the Podman installation. Confirm that `rootless` is among the active security features.

- **Configuring User Namespace**

If rootless configuration is not active, the user namespace may need to be configured. Set up the user mapping in /etc/subuid and /etc/subgid:

```
user:100000:65536
```

This entry indicates that the user is allowed a UID range starting from 100000 and spanning 65536 IDs. The configuration allows Podman to reallocate UIDs and GIDs for containers started by this user, providing a secure namespace for rootless operation.

- **Running Containers in Rootless Mode**

With the correct configuration in place, running containers in rootless mode is straightforward and follows the same command patterns as root mode, leveraging Podman's Docker-compatible CLI.

```
podman run -d --name rootless_nginx -p 8080:80 nginx
```

This command initiates a container named `rootless_nginx` mapped to port 8080 on the host. Despite appearing to have root privileges, within the container context, the operations are executed under the invoking user's privileges. The container still has root privileges in its namespace, allowing typical administrative operations without impacting the actual host security boundaries.

• Networking Configurations and Challenges

One of the complexities in rootless container operation pertains to networking. Since rootless containers do not have host-level root privileges, they encounter limitations with certain network operations that require root access, such as binding to privileged ports (e.g., below 1024).

Podman facilitates this by automatically configuring network namespaces for containers started in rootless mode. Utilizing slirp4netns provides user-space networking for containers, thus enabling network connectivity without root.

To expose a rootless container to a host's higher ports, redirect those ports following network best practices:

```
# Expose container's port 80 to host port 8080
podman run -d --name web_service -p 8080:80 my_web_image
```

When dealing with rootless containers, the network stack operations run in user space, which may impact performance under heavy network loads, but the trade-off is enhanced security and operational independence.

• Advantages and Considerations of Rootless Mode

There are several compelling advantages related to rootless mode:

- Enhanced Security: Operating containers without root eliminates significant attack vectors associated with elevated privileges. It provides an assurance layer on multi-tenant systems where users share host resources.

- Development and Testing: Developers benefit from the rootless mode by duplicating production environments on local machines without administrative privileges, streamlining development and testing workflows.

- Ease of Use: Users can install and operate Podman within their home directory without elevated installation permissions, facilitating container experimentation and learning without altering system settings.

- User-Space Network Configuration: Encapsulating network configurations in user space ensures that network changes remain isolated to the user's namespace.

- **Challenges and Limitations**

Despite its security and ease-of-use benefits, the rootless mode incurs some limitations:

- Suboptimal Network Performance: Networking in user space (slirp4netns) may decrease performance due to additional overhead compared to privileged host networking.

- Complex Usability: Users must be aware of the constraints of host resources accessible in rootless mode, impacting some performance optimization or resource usage scenarios.

- File Permissions: File handling needs extra attention, considering UID/GID mappings different than what appears in the container or host settings.

- **Advanced Configuration and Fine-Tuning**

For users requiring advanced setup or overcoming certain limitations inherent to rootless operation, Podman supports configuration customizations:

- CNI (Container Network Interface) Plugin Configuration: Advanced users might explore configuring CNI plugins, which allow defining network layouts offering more flexibility and performance gains over default user-space networking.

- Systemd Integration: To enhance service management for rootless containers, integrate Podman with systemd within user space. This permits reprovisioning containers as system services without root dependency.

```
[Unit]
Description=Podman rootless nginx container
Wants=network-online.target
After=network-online.target

[Service]
User=container_user
ExecStart=/usr/bin/podman run --rm -d --name nginx -p 8080:80 nginx
ExecStop=/usr/bin/podman stop -t 2 nginx
Restart=always

[Install]
WantedBy=default.target
```

This unit file provides an example of integrating a rootless Podman service with systemd, ensuring the container executes with user privileges as a systemd-managed service.

- **Future of Rootless Containers**

With the growing need for secure and efficient containerization solutions, rootless containers are steadily gaining traction as viable mainstream alternatives, especially in security-constrained environments or resource-shared physical machines where compromise of minimal privilege is vital. Continuous enhancements to user-space tools, as evidenced by recent updates to Podman's capabilities, signal an optimistic trajectory toward expanding rootless container functionality to match traditional container operations' power and flexibility.

Integrating emerging technologies alongside rootless container advancements, such as intelligent user-space networking enhancements or automated security tooling, promises to redefine containerized workloads and their management paradigms.

In environments where security considerations are paramount, adopting Podman's rootless mode explicitly aligns with best security practices, offering a robust, user-friendly alternative to traditional root-reliant container solutions. As the industry embraces least privilege principles, Podman's rootless capabilities position it as a forward-looking choice for secure and scalable container management.

7.3. Container Health Checks and Monitoring

Ensuring that containers operate efficiently and reliably is fundamental to deploying scalable and resilient services. Docker introduced the concept of health checks, and Podman inherits this feature to allow administrators to automate the verification of container states. Health checks provide a mechanism for testing whether the application running inside a container is healthy and capable of handling requests. This capability, combined with monitoring, enables a systematic approach to maintaining container environments.

- **Understanding Container Health Checks:** Health checks in containers serve as guards over the application processes. They periodically evaluate predefined conditions and metrics to ensure that the containerized application is functioning as intended. A health check comprises a command or script that runs inside the container, checking for conditions indicative of the application's health, such as responsiveness to requests, availability of a necessary service, or correctness of the application's behavior.

186

- **Implementing Health Checks in Podman:** With Podman, health checks can be configured during container creation using the `--health-cmd` parameter. This parameter allows specification of the test script or command that Podman should execute to verify container health.

```
podman run -d \
  --name=my_app \
  --health-cmd="curl --fail http://localhost:8080/ || exit
1" \
  --health-interval=30s \
  my_app_image
```

In this example, a health check is set for the my_app container. Every 30 seconds, Podman runs the `curl` command to ensure that the application responds as expected on port 8080. If `curl` fails (e.g., the server is down or returns an error), the health check will exit with a non-zero status, marking the container as unhealthy.

- **Configuring Health Check Parameters:** Beyond the health command itself, several parameters customize health checks:

  - `--health-interval`: Specifies the interval between health checks. The default is 30 seconds.

  - `--health-timeout`: Sets a timeout period for the health check command. Should the command exceed this time without completing, it is considered failed.

  - `--health-retries`: Defines the number of consecutive failures before marking a container as unhealthy.

  These parameters enable tailored deployments based on application behavior or resource constraints, offering flexible strategies to maintain their health proactively.

- **Health Check Management and Insights:** An important aspect of health checks lies in managing their results and deriving insights for better container orchestration. Administrators

187

should ensure adequate monitoring is in place to react to health check failures, whether by restarting containers, triggering alerts, or scaling applications dynamically.

Check the status of a container's health with Podman:

```
podman inspect --format "{{.State.Health.Status}}" my_app
```

This command will output the current health status, which could be healthy, unhealthy, or starting. By analyzing this information, administrators can take appropriate strategic actions, automating responses in coordination with orchestration tools.

- **Monitoring Container Health with Podman:** In addition to health checks, deploying effective monitoring mechanisms is essential for managing container lifecycles. Monitoring encompasses tracking key performance metrics and logs, crucial for diagnosing issues and enhancing reliability.

  Podman offers various tooling extensions and integrations to implement comprehensive monitoring solutions, including:

  - **Podman Logs:** View real-time logs to analyze container performance and error messaging.
    ```
    podman logs my_app
    ```

  - **Podman Stats:** This feature provides real-time metrics of running containers, detailing CPU, memory usage, and I/O statistics.
    ```
    podman stats --no-stream
    ```

  - **Integration with Nagios/Prometheus/Grafana:** Advanced monitoring tools like Prometheus can be configured to scrape metrics from containers, providing real-time visualization and alerting via tools like Grafana.

188

- **Use Case: Monitoring with Prometheus:** To monitor a container's performance more systematically, consider integrating Prometheus alongside your running Podman containers. Prometheus requires an exporter to be present within the container, capable of exposing metrics in a Prometheus-compatible format.

  - **Exporter Configuration:** Embed a Prometheus-compatible exporter in the container or run it alongside the application. For example, the node_exporter is commonly used:

    ```
    podman run -d \
        --name=node_exporter \
        -p 9100:9100 \
        quay.io/prometheus/node-exporter
    ```

  - **Prometheus Setup:** Configure Prometheus to scrape metrics from the exported endpoints. Define a prometheus.yml configuration file:

    ```
    scrape_configs:
      - job_name: 'node_exporter'
        static_configs:
          - targets: ['localhost:9100']
    ```

  - **Start Prometheus:**

    ```
    podman run -d \
        --name=prometheus \
        -v /path/to/prometheus.yml:/etc/prometheus/
    prometheus.yml \
        -p 9090:9090 \
        prom/prometheus
    ```

  - **Visualizing with Grafana:** Lastly, set up Grafana to visualize the metrics dashboards conducive to understanding application loads, resource utilization, and other critical factors.

189

- **Beyond Basics: Proactive Monitoring with Alerts:** Effective container management transcends simply performing health checks and collecting metrics: it involves proactive monitoring with responsive alerts. Here are strategies to enhance monitoring efficacy:

  - Implement threshold-based alerts; configure Prometheus or a similar tool to trigger SMS/email alerts if performance metrics breach predefined limits.

  - Utilize anomaly detection algorithms that analyze metric patterns, identifying unusual operational behavior suggesting undiagnosed issues.

  - Optimize data retention policies by ensuring long-term storage of key metrics, allowing in-depth historical analysis for performance tuning.

- **Cultivating an Active Monitoring Culture:** Improving monitoring culture encompasses regular refinement and iteration of your methodologies. Regularly review and update health checks to address changes in application behavior, incorporate feedback from operations teams to fine-tune alerting mechanisms, and promote continuous learning within your team to leverage monitoring data effectively.

Analyzing health check and monitoring data empowers operations and development teams to preemptively address application improvements and infrastructure optimization, positioning containerized environments for high efficiency and reliability. Embrace a culture of observability and continuous improvement to maximize the operational and strategic benefits of containerization with Podman, ensuring robust service levels across the board.

7.4. Managing Container Resources

Efficient resource management is a critical aspect of operating containerized environments, particularly in production settings where optimizing for performance, cost, and responsiveness is paramount. Podman, like many container runtime tools, provides robust mechanisms for managing resource allocation among containers, enabling administrators to finely tune their deployments to meet specific operational needs. The goal is to maximize efficient resource utilization while ensuring applications remain performant under varying workloads.

Container resource management in Podman involves configuring constraints and setting limits on CPU, memory, and other system resources. Adequate planning and resource definition help ensure fair distribution, prevent resource starvation, and maintain isolated execution environments effectively.

- **CPU and Memory Limits**: These define the upper bounds of CPU cycles and memory a container can consume, preventing any individual container from monopolizing system resources.

- **Resource Reservation**: Ensures containers have guaranteed access to a non-zero amount of system resources, pertinent during high system load.

- **Cgroups (Control Groups)**: A Linux kernel feature that provides resource accounting and limitation, enabling fine-grained control over system resources for containers.

- **Namespaces**: Segregate resources to ensure isolated execution environments, critical for security and stability.

Configuring Resource Limits with Podman

Podman utilizes the concept of resource constraints to limit the impact any individual container has on host system resources. Here's how to configure resource limits during container instantiation:

```
podman run -d \
  --name resource_limited_container \
  --memory=512m \
  --cpus=2 \
  my_application_image
```

In this configuration, the 'resource_limited_container' is constrained to a limit of 512 megabytes of memory and restricted to using at most two CPUs. These settings ensure that no matter the load or demands placed on the application, it cannot exceed these predefined boundaries, safeguarding other applications from being adversely affected.

Detailed Resource Constraints

Memory Constraints: Memory limitations cap the memory usage for a container, vital for preventing applications from consuming excessive host memory. Podman supports both hard ('–memory') and swap ('–memory-swap') limits.

- **Hard Limit**: The maximum memory allocation.

- **Swap Limit**: Total combined memory and swap usage for containers.

```
podman run -d \
  --name mem_swap_limited \
  --memory=256m \
  --memory-swap=512m \
  my_application_image
```

CPU Constraints: CPU usage can be regulated by limiting the number of CPUs available or defining a specific CPU share. Use the '–cpus' flag to specify the maximum CPU resources allowed.

- **CPU Quota**: Podman provides '–cpu-quota' and '–cpu-period' to control scheduling of CPU resources.

Consider the following example where CPU limitations are defined using quota and period:

```
podman run -d \
  --name cpu_advanced_limited \
  --cpu-period=100000 \
  --cpu-quota=50000 \
  my_application_image
```

Here, the container is allowed to consume half of the time of a single CPU.

Persistent Resource Management

Podman's flexibility extends to managing resources in a persistent manner, allowing configurations to be maintained across container reboots. When updating configurations, ensure the 'podman update' command reflects any amendments:

```
podman update --memory=1g --cpus=3 existing_container
```

Persistent management ensures consistency in operational deployments, maintaining optimized resource confinements even through container restarts or migrations.

Resource Monitoring and Adjustment

Proper resource management also entails monitoring consumption patterns and adjusting allocations dynamically based on performance metrics and workload requirements. Podman facilitates direct access to container statistics, aiding in responsive management.

```
podman stats --no-stream
```

This command provides insights into CPU usage, memory utilization, network bandwidth, and more. Use these insights to assess whether current resource allocations are optimal or require adjustments, addressing bottlenecks proactively.

Automating Resource Management

Automating resource management with scripts or integrated platforms simplifies maintaining equilibrium across distributed environments:

- **Autoscaling**: Implement scripts that adjust resource allocations based on thresholds or triggers from monitoring tools.

- **Policy-Based Management**: Define policies where containers receive dynamic resource allocations based on predefined criteria.

- **Container Orchestration Solutions**: Use orchestrators like Kubernetes, which inherently manage resource distribution among clustered deployments, leveraging native features for horizontal and vertical scaling, ensuring fine-grained resource control, and optimizing container densities.

Challenges and Best Practices

While Podman offers robust resource management capabilities, certain challenges and best practices exist:

- **Balancing Resource Utilization vs Performance**: Overly aggressive constraints could throttle applications, impacting performance. Aim for a balance that allows peak utilization without over-provisioning.

- **Monitoring Overhead**: Resource monitoring, while beneficial, incurs system overhead. Evaluate the trade-off to strike a balance between resource usage for monitoring and running application tasks.

- **Cgroup Configuration**: Misconfigured cgroups may result in performance penalties, thus necessitating careful cgroup setup tailored for the specific workload characteristics.

- **Regular Reviews**: Continuously review resource utilization patterns, adapting strategies to address changes in application demands or underlying hardware capabilities.

Future trends in resource management include AI-driven resource allocation and predictive scaling, promising streamlined operations by aligning resource distribution dynamically with workload forecasting. Integrating machine learning models that interpret historical data alongside real-time metrics fosters smarter decision-making processes in resource allocations, minimizing human intervention and achieving maximum potential from available infrastructure.

Effective container resource management with Podman involves a comprehensive understanding of container resource settings, active performance monitoring, and familiarity with advanced configuration possibilities. Adopting automated and policy-driven approaches, combined with modern technologies, ensures optimal performance, resource utilization, and cost management across containerized environments. By leveraging these capabilities, organizations can increase service reliability and maintain a competitive edge through efficient resource deployment and management strategies.

7.5. Pod Management with Podman

In containerized application architectures, especially those conforming to microservices principles, managing multiple related containers efficiently is crucial. Here, the concept of "pods" becomes instrumental, providing a cohesive mechanism to group and orchestrate multiple containers sharing the same network namespace and volumes.

Podman introduces robust capabilities for pod management, paralleling Kubernetes' abstractions, which facilitate sophisticated multi-container deployments that simulate a service-oriented architecture within a single node.

Introducing Pods: The Logical Grouping of Containers

A pod in Podman represents one or more containers that are tightly coupled, sharing the network namespace and storage options. This tight integration supports scenarios where containers within a pod need to communicate locally without network restrictions or need synchronized restart policies.

Benefits of using pods in Podman include:

- **Simplified Networking**: Containers within a pod can communicate via `localhost`, eliminating the need for complex networking configurations.

- **Resource Sharing**: Sharing volumes and network namespaces aids in cost-effective resource utilization strategies.

- **Unified Lifecycle Management**: Pods allow the grouping of lifecycle commands, enabling a centralized approach to starting, stopping, or deleting multiple interconnected containers.

Creating and Managing Pods

To leverage pods effectively in Podman, understanding how to create and manage them through the command-line interface is key.

Creating a Pod

Creating a pod using Podman involves specifying resources shared between constituent containers. Here's the basic syntax to create a new pod:

```
podman pod create --name my_pod --share net --publish 8080:80
```

In this example, `my_pod` is created to share networking capabilities. It exposes host port 8080 to container port 80, setting the stage for the pod's internal services that rely on network communication.

Adding Containers to Pods

Once a pod is created, containers can be deployed within the pod to form interrelated application units. Existing containers can also be linked to a newly created pod:

```
podman run -dt --pod my_pod my_web_server
podman run -dt --pod my_pod my_database
```

These commands add two different application components—`my_web_server` and `my_database`—into `my_pod`, allowing them to operate collaboratively, sharing network and volume space as necessary.

Advanced Features and Pod Configuration

Pods in Podman support advanced functionality aimed at enhancing deployment scenarios and flexible configuration management across various operational contexts.

Pod-Level Resource Management

Similar to individual container constraints, pods support resource allocations, ensuring all containers within follow predefined limits. This enhances both security and performance guarantees across tightly coupled container groups.

```
podman pod create --name my_pod --memory=1g --cpus=2
```

This command restricts the entire pod to utilize a maximum of 1 GB memory and 2 CPUs cumulatively, assuring fair resource utilization while preventing individual containers within the pod from over-consuming resources.

Inspecting Pods

To get insights into pod configurations, states, and associated containers, Podman provides robust inspection commands:

```
podman pod inspect my_pod
```

The output provides detailed information about the pod's state, including container IDs, networking configuration, and resource allocation, aiding in pinpointing issues or configuration mismatches.

Pod Network and Volume Sharing

The pivotal feature of pods encompasses network and volume sharing among containers. Shared networking implies intra-pod communication using `localhost`, effectively bypassing the need for external IP assignment.

Internal Pod Communication

Containers within a pod operate in the same network namespace, increasing efficiency of service interaction:

```
# Assuming my_web_server listens on port 80
curl http://localhost:8080/internal_resource
```

This command demonstrates an intra-pod call between service containers, emphasizing how Podman simplifies inter-service communication through shared namespaces.

Volume Sharing

Volume sharing allows containers to read/write on common data storage, facilitating the synchronization of persistent data among service components:

```
podman pod create --name with_shared_volume --volume /shareddata:/srv
```

```
    /data
```

During pod creation, the --volume flag mounts the host directory /shareddata as /srv/data within the pod, ensuring file-based operations remain synchronized across container instances.

Pod Lifecycle Management

As an operational enhancement, Podman pods simplify lifecycle management commands over grouped containers, synchronizing their operational state:

```
podman pod start my_pod
podman pod stop my_pod
podman pod restart my_pod
podman pod rm my_pod
```

These unified commands enhance operational efficiency, particularly within environments employing automated deployment strategies or CI/CD pipelines.

Integration with Systemd

For long-running pods, integrating with systemd provides capabilities to manage pods as system services, enhancing their robustness and integration with host-based security policies:

```
[Unit]
Description=Podman Pod my_pod
Wants=network-online.target
After=network-online.target

[Service]
Restart=on-failure
ExecStart=/usr/bin/podman pod start my_pod
ExecStop=/usr/bin/podman pod stop -t 10 my_pod

[Install]
WantedBy=multi-user.target
```

System administrators can define systemd units like the above, enabling pods to be part of the host's initiation routine, providing seamless startup and shutdown processes aligned with system restarts or policies.

Best Practices for Pod Management

Effective pod management involves several best practices, ensuring optimized resource usage, security, and application performance:

- **Avoid Overloading Pods**: Limit the number of containers per pod to accommodate the most logical grouping relative to resource isolation, managing complexity, and avoiding point failures.

- **Ensure Clear Network Policies**: Define explicit networking policies to ensure pods isolate internal and external traffic as necessary, safeguarding against unauthorized interventions.

- **Align Resource Limits with Load**: Balance pod resource limits with expected loads to prevent throttling, underscoring vigilant monitoring and optimizations based on historical application usage.

- **Consistent Configuration Management**: Employ infrastructure as code and configuration management tools for declarative and consistent pod definitions, ensuring replicability across environments.

Mastering pod management in Podman empowers developers and operations teams to deploy complex applications composed of discrete service elements effectively, allocating computational resources cohesively and maximizing interoperability efficiencies. By leveraging these comprehensive pod management strategies, organizations can streamline application delivery and operation, achieving an agile, scalable, and resilient infrastructure suitable for modern, dynamic applications. With continuous enhancements, Podman and its pod management capabilities represent a future-ready architecture seamlessly fitting into diverse deployment ecosystems.

7.6. Integrating Podman with Systemd

System and service management are integral to ensuring that applications run smoothly and efficiently. The systemd initialization system provides a comprehensive service management suite essential for modern Linux distributions, facilitating service management, system resources delegation, and process resource consumption control. Integrating Podman with systemd extends these capabilities to Docker-compatible containers, streamlining their deployment, management, and monitoring. This section explores approaches to integrate Podman with systemd for managing containers as first-class system services.

Understanding the Synergy: Podman + Systemd

Podman, known for its daemonless architecture, leverages systemd's robust capabilities to ensure containerized environments operate in harmony with the broader system management framework, providing:

- **System Reliability**: Automating container initialization, monitoring, and recovery, supporting graceful restarts upon failures or system reboots.

- **Resource Management**: Seamless integration into the cgroups management, enabling optimized resource utilization.

- **Compliance and Security**: Aligning with host security policies and leveraging service isolation, ensuring adherence to a system's security posture.

Basic Setup for Podman and Systemd

The integration process commences by understanding how to translate container operations into unit files—small snippets of configuration recognized by systemd to handle service behaviors.

Generating Systemd Unit Files

Podman simplifies the creation of systemd unit files using the 'generate systemd' command, automating the configuration necessary to manage containers as systemd services.

```
podman run -d --name my_service my_image

podman generate systemd --name my_service --files --new
```

The command above generates a unit file encapsulating the necessary configuration directives. The '—new' flag ensures the service initiates from a clean state, irrespective of existing file system overlays, enhancing reliability.

```
# my_service.service
[Unit]
Description=Podman container-my_service.service
Documentation=man:podman-generate-systemd(1)
Wants=network-online.target
After=network-online.target

[Service]
Restart=on-failure
ExecStart=/usr/bin/podman start my_service
ExecStop=/usr/bin/podman stop -t 10 my_service
PIDFile=/run/podman-%n.pid

[Install]
WantedBy=multi-user.target
```

This unit file describes essential service components, including dependencies ('Wants' and 'After' directives), service behavior, restart policies, and initialization directives.

Deploying and Managing Systemd Services

Once generated, incorporate the unit file into the systemd environment to deploy Podman-managed services seamlessly.

Enabling and Starting the Service

Move the unit file to the systemd directory and utilize systemd commands to enable and start the service.

```
sudo mv my_service.service /etc/systemd/system/
sudo systemctl enable my_service.service
sudo systemctl start my_service.service
```

These commands move the service file into the appropriate system location and register it with systemd, marking it to automatically start on boot and initiate immediately.

Monitoring Systemd-managed Containers

Systemd provides a slew of utilities for monitoring and logging service status, enabling detailed analytical insights into service operations and disruptions.

```
systemctl status my_service.service
```

The command above provides details on the status of `my_service`, including recent logs and service activity metrics, which are vital for diagnosing issues and ensuring continuous operational alignment.

Advanced Systemd Features for Container Services

Beyond basic start-stop routines, systemd avails a plethora of advanced management capabilities that can be leveraged to optimize Podman service integrations.

Timer Units and Scheduling

Systemd's timer units replace cron jobs, offering more sophisticated scheduling options directly integrated with the service management framework. A container could be started specifically at pre-defined intervals:

```
# my_service.timer
[Unit]
Description=Run my_service every day

[Timer]
OnCalendar=daily
Persistent=true

[Install]
WantedBy=timers.target
```

Activate the timer unit alongside the main service:

```
sudo systemctl enable my_service.timer
sudo systemctl start my_service.timer
```

Using this configuration, `my_service` is triggered daily by systemd, making time-based service management more intuitive and aligned with system resources.

Secure Service Operations

Enhancing the security of service operations is made easier due to systemd's integrated security hardening options. These include restricting file system access, isolating network connections, and controlling process permissions:

```
[Service]
ProtectSystem=full
ProtectHome=yes
NoNewPrivileges=true
```

These directives ensure that the subsystems interacting with container processes have the minimum necessary privileges, crucial for maintaining service integrity within shared infrastructures.

Challenges and Best Practices

While integrating Podman with systemd promises ample advantages, understanding potential challenges and adhering to best practices ensures smooth operations:

- **Maintaining Configuration Consistency**: Regularly reviewing systemd unit configurations mitigates the risk of drifts in service behavior due to unauthorized changes.

- **Resource Allocation Fidelity**: Monitor and adjust resource constraints as necessary to avoid throttling, leveraging cgroups efficiently within service definitions.

- **Testing Service Dependencies**: Exercising thorough testing before deployment ensures that service dependencies resolved through 'Wants' or 'After' are valid and available.

- **Documentation and Logging**: Utilize systemd's inherently detailed logging ('journalctl') for documenting service operations, supporting audits and compliance objectives.

Integrating with Ecosystem and Future Trends

As service management becomes more sophisticated, adopting emerging trends that enhance systemd and Podman's combination is worthwhile:

- **Service Mesh Integration**: Leverage service meshes to facilitate communication between deployed services at scale.

- **Container Orchestration Synergies**: Where feasible, integrate orchestration layers like Kubernetes alongside Podman for distributed container management.

- **AI and Automation**: Incorporating AI-driven insights into systemd timers aids in predictive scaling, and optimal service provisioning strategies ensure seamless user experiences.

Chapter 8

Podman Compose: Orchestrating Multi-Container Applications

This chapter covers the orchestration of multi-container applications using Podman Compose, detailing the setup and use of Compose files for service definition. It provides instructions on deploying, managing, and scaling applications and explores networking configurations for seamless inter-container communication. Readers gain insights into efficiently updating services without downtime, enabling robust application deployment and management. By mastering Podman Compose, users can deploy complex applications with ease and precision, optimizing resource utilization and ensuring operational continuity across containers.

8.1. Understanding Multi-Container Applications

In contemporary application development, leveraging containerization is pivotal due to its numerous advantages in terms of scalability, agility, and resource management. The concept of multi-container applications is a natural extension of this approach, allowing complex applications to be architected with the separation of concerns in mind. This section examines the fundamental facets of multi-container applications, their advantages, and the challenges associated with their deployment and management.

Multi-Container Architecture:

A multi-container application consists of several interconnected containers, each performing a specific role within an overall system. This model adheres to the microservices architecture, where each service is autonomous and communicates via APIs or messaging protocols. Typically, such applications encompass a variety of services, including but not limited to web servers, database systems, caching solutions, and background processing units.

Orchestration and Management:

The deployment and orchestration of multi-container applications are managed using tools like Kubernetes, Docker Compose, and Podman Compose. These systems handle the lifecycle of containers, easing the management of scaling, networking, load balancing, and service updates. Podman Compose, specifically, is designed to function seamlessly with Podman's compatibility features with Docker, ensuring a smooth transition and integration in existing workflows.

Advantages of Multi-Container Applications:

- **Modularity and Reusability:** Each container encapsulates a specific service, allowing multiple instances of the same service to run independently. This modularity facilitates the maintenance and upgrading of individual services without impacting the entire application.

- **Scalability:** Multi-container applications can scale horizontally, adding more containers for services that require additional computational resources. For example, during increased traffic, more instances of a web server container can be launched to distribute the load.

- **Fault Isolation:** Problems within a single service (container) do not necessarily propagate to other components, reducing the application's total downtime risk. If one service fails, mechanisms are in place to restart the affected containers automatically.

- **Consistent Environments:** Containers provide uniform environments across various stages of production, testing, and development. This consistency is essential for identifying bugs, optimizing performance, and ensuring the reliability of application functionality.

- **Efficient Resource Utilization:** Containers run isolated processes, share the same OS kernel, and often require fewer resources than virtual machines, allowing more efficient use of underlying hardware.

Networking and Communication:

Inter-container communication involves networking solutions that allow containers within the same application to communicate seamlessly.

In Podman Compose, several networking options facilitate this interaction:

- **Bridge Networks:** Virtual networks allowing communication between containers on the same host.

- **Host Network:** Containers share the host's network stack, enabling performance optimization at the cost of namespace separation.

- **Container Linking:** Containers communicate through dedicated environment variables and open ports, easing direct linkage.

```
version: '3.7'
services:
  webapp:
    image: nginx:alpine
    networks:
      - frontend

  data_service:
    image: postgres:alpine
    networks:
      - backend

networks:
  frontend:
    driver: bridge
  backend:
    driver: bridge
```

In this YAML configuration, a Podman Compose file defines two distinct services, webapp and data_service, each using different bridge networks to illustrate inter-service isolation.

Persistent Storage:

By design, containers are ephemeral, and any data generated is lost after the container is stopped or deleted. This can be suboptimal for

210

stateful services like databases. Using persistent storage options, such as volumes and bind mounts, is vital:

```
version: '3.7'
services:
  database:
    image: postgres:alpine
    volumes:
      - dbdata:/var/lib/postgresql/data

volumes:
  dbdata:
```

This configuration demonstrates creating a volume dbdata to persist data across container restarts. Volumes help maintain data integrity and durability in multi-container architectures.

Security Considerations:

Security is a crucial aspect of multi-container applications. Enabling stringent access controls and implementing best security practices help mitigate risks:

- **Use of Non-Root Users:** Running services as non-root users within a container minimizes security vulnerabilities.

- **Network Policies:** Restrict inter-container communications to necessary paths only, using network policies effectively.

- **Image Security:** Regularly scanning and updating container images to include the latest security patches.

Challenges and Solutions:

Although multi-container applications present several benefits, they introduce complexities:

- **Complexity in Management:** The increase in the number of services and interactions enhances the management complexity.

Using orchestration tools simplifies these tasks by automating coherence between various components.

- **Debugging and Logging:** Increased decomposition complicates tracing bugs. Implementing centralized logging and monitoring tools, such as ELK stack or Prometheus, helps in tracking container activity and diagnosing issues.

- **Resource Management:** Ensuring adequate resources are provisioned for each service without wastage. Resource constraints can be managed by setting appropriate limits on CPU and memory usage within the Podman Compose configuration.

```
version: '3.7'
services:
  compute:
    image: python:alpine
    deploy:
      resources:
        limits:
          cpus: '0.50'
          memory: 512M
```

Including a `deploy` section with resource constraints ensures optimal performance without unnecessary resource consumption.

Adopting a multi-container approach unleashes the full potential of containerization, paving the way for scalable, flexible, and efficient application delivery. This foundation enables improved operational management and service reliability while embracing modern architectural paradigms.

8.2. Getting Started with Podman Compose

Podman Compose is a valuable tool for managing and orchestrating multi-container applications. Similar to Docker Compose, it facilitates the definition and running of complex applications using a declarative configuration file. This section explores the essentials of getting started with Podman Compose, including the installation requirements and the foundational concepts needed to effectively utilize the tool.

Installation and Setup:

The initial step in leveraging Podman Compose involves installing Podman itself, along with Podman Compose. Podman provides a Docker-compatible CLI interface and a comprehensive, daemonless container management experience. The installation process may vary based on the operating system but generally includes similar procedures across various Unix-like systems.

- **1. Podman Installation:** Podman can be installed from the default package manager on most systems. For instance, on a Fedora system, the following command installs Podman:

```
sudo dnf install podman
```

  On Ubuntu systems:

```
sudo apt update
sudo apt install podman
```

- **2. Installing Podman Compose:** Podman Compose is a Python-based utility that can be installed using pip, the Python package manager. Ensure Python and pip are installed on your system, then execute:

```
pip install podman-compose
```

  Post-installation, verify that both Podman and Podman Compose are correctly installed by confirming their versions:

```
podman --version
podman-compose --version
```

213

Configuration and Environment Setup:

For Podman Compose operations, ensure that the Podman service is correctly configured and that the networking components are appropriately set. Podman operates either as root or rootless. Rootless mode is preferred for increased security, although it requires additional setup for network configurations.

In rootless mode, users must configure a slirp4netns network or use a system-wide CNI network. Enabling CNI network support enhances networking capabilities for inter-container communication.

```
sudo systemctl enable --now podman
```

Additionally, ensure that `podman-compose` has access to the relevant networking functions and directories, usually managed by environment setup in your shell's profile.

Basic Concepts and Workflow:

Podman Compose operates using YAML configuration files, which outline services, networks, and volumes necessary for the multi-container application. The fundamental workflow involves creating a `docker-compose.yml` or simply a `compose.yml` file that specifies all application services.

An essential configuration might look like this:

```
version: '3.7'
services:
  my_service:
    image: busybox
    command: echo 'Hello, Podman Compose'
```

In this file, version dictates the syntax version of the Compose file, while services define containers. This simplicity exemplifies a basic

214

setup; however, real-world applications typically require additional configurations for networking and persistent storage.

Running a Podman Compose Application:

Once the configuration file is complete, launching the application is straightforward using the Podman Compose CLI:

```
podman-compose up -d
```

The -d flag specifies a detached mode, allowing the terminal to remain free for additional commands. To shut down the application, utilize:

```
podman-compose down
```

This command stops all running containers and removes networks defined in the configuration file. It does not remove volumes or images unless specified explicitly.

Integration with Existing Docker Workflows:

A significant advantage of Podman Compose lies in its compatibility with existing Docker Compose workflows. This compatibility enables organizations and developers transitioning from Docker to Podman to continue utilizing their existing Compose files with minimal adjustments.

For seamless integration, the existing Docker Compose YAML files are usually sufficient with minor modifications. These alterations typically involve changing service names or network configurations specific to Podman. However, features and tags used solely by Docker may necessitate refactoring.

```
version: '3.7'
services:
  api_gateway:
    image: nginx:alpine
    ports:
      - "8080:80"
    depends_on:
```

```
        - backend
    backend:
      image: python:3.8-slim
```

This example demonstrates a typical setup involving an API gateway and backend service, originally designed for Docker but adapted for use with Podman Compose.

Limitations and Considerations:

Although Podman Compose provides analogous functionality to Docker Compose, some limitations and considerations include:

- **Rootless Networking:** Special attention is required for rootless mode network compatibility, as networking capabilities differ from Docker Compose's default CNI.

- **Resource Constraints:** Ensure adequate system resources and permissions, especially in rootless scenarios.

- **Available Plugins and Extensions:** Some Docker plugins may not be directly transferable to Podman, requiring alternative approaches or tool adaptations.

Podman Compose offers a robust solution for handling container orchestration when integrated with modern architectures. Through careful setup and configuration, developers can leverage this tool to deploy efficient and scalable multi-container applications while benefiting from Podman's enhanced security model and Docker compatibility.

8.3.   Defining Services in a Compose File

The core function of Podman Compose is to facilitate the orchestration of multi-container applications through defining services, networks, and volumes in a YAML-based configuration file. Understanding how to accurately define services within a Compose file is crucial for leveraging the full potential of Podman Compose. This section delves into the components and attributes necessary to define robust services within a Compose file, examining essential parameters and configurations to optimize deployment and management of containerized applications.

Service definitions are the building blocks that represent individual containers running a specific image. Each service specification includes several key components: the image to run, runtime configurations, command execution, environment variables, port mappings, volumes, and dependencies.

```
version: '3.7'

services:
  app:
    image: nginx:alpine
```

This elementary example specifies a service named app using the nginx:alpine image.

The image parameter specifies the container image, which may be located in a public registry such as Docker Hub or in a private repository. Alternatively, images can be constructed from a local Dockerfile using the build directive.

```
version: '3.7'

services:
  customservice:
    build:
      context: ./app
      dockerfile: Dockerfile
```

In this scenario, the build section indicates the context directory and the specific Dockerfile used to generate the image. This flexibility is beneficial when tailoring images with custom configurations or dependencies.

217

The command attribute enables the overriding of the default command specified by the image. More intricate setup procedures often require specific entry commands and argument pass-throughs.

```
version: '3.7'

services:
  webserver:
    image: node:14
    command: ["npm", "start"]
```

This specification ensures that the npm start command is executed upon container initialization, triggering the Node.js application contained within.

In Podman Compose, incorporating environment variables is crucial for dynamic configuration and ensuring flexibility across various deployment environments.

```
version: '3.7'

services:
  backend:
    image: php:7.4-cli
    environment:
      - DB_HOST=database
      - DB_PORT=3306
```

Defining key-value pairs within the environment section injects necessary variables into the container environment, influencing application configurations.

Inter-container communication and external service availability necessitate appropriate port mapping. Using the ports parameter, external ports are associated with corresponding internal container ports.

```
version: '3.7'

services:
  app:
    image: httpd:alpine
    ports:
      - "8080:80"
```

This example maps port 80 inside the container to port 8080 on the host machine, allowing HTTP requests from outside to reach the web service hosted within the app container.

Persistence of data beyond container lifecycles is achieved through volumes. Volumes can be defined and named globally within the Compose file, ensuring data durability and cross-service accessibility.

```
version: '3.7'

services:
  database:
    image: mysql:5.7
    volumes:
      - dbdata:/var/lib/mysql

volumes:
  dbdata:
```

Here, `dbdata` is identified as a named volume persisting the MySQL database files, maintaining state across container restarts or rebuilds.

Service interdependencies often dictate the order of initialization. The `depends_on` attribute provides control over startup sequences, ensuring respective services are available as needed.

```
version: '3.7'

services:
  api:
    image: flask:latest
    depends_on:
      - webapp
  webapp:
    image: nginx:alpine
```

Here, the `api` service depends on the `webapp` service. Podman handles the initialization process accordingly, albeit without enforcing complex orchestration beyond starting order.

Beyond basic port mappings, Podman Compose enables more advanced networking setups, facilitating intricate inter-service communication and network isolation.

```
version: '3.7'

services:
  front_service:
    image: nginx
    networks:
      - frontnet

  back_service:
    image: node
    networks:
      - backnet

networks:
  frontnet:
    driver: bridge
  backnet:
    driver: bridge
```

This file establishes two networks, `frontnet` and `backnet`, separating network traffic based on function, a practice that enhances security and organizes service interactions.

Within complex networks, distinct hostname assignments and service aliases facilitate the ease of domain-based service access.

```
version: '3.7'

services:
  web:
    image: httpd
    hostname: myserver
    networks:
      app_net:
        aliases:
          - webapp.local

networks:
  app_net:
```

The web service is identifiable within the app_net network as myserver, utilizing `webapp.local` as an alias, simplifying domain-based service interactions within the network.

Efficient resource management is achieved through explicit resource constraints within a Compose file, preventing resource exhaustion and optimizing execution environments.

```
version: '3.7'

services:
  compute:
    image: python:alpine
    deploy:
      resources:
        limits:
          cpus: '2.00'
          memory: 2G
```

This configuration sets a cap on available CPUs and memory, ensuring the `compute` service operates within predefined resource boundaries, preventing overconsumption and maintaining system stability.

The capacity to define services within a Compose file endows developers with a powerful tool to manage containerized applications effectively. Through leveraging the array of features offered by Podman Compose—ranging from simple configurations to elaborate orchestrations—users can create adaptable and efficient solutions, accommodating varied application demands. This detailed understanding enables an improved deployment strategy, aligning closely with organizational goals and technical objectives.

8.4. Running and Managing Multi-Container Applications

Running and managing multi-container applications using Podman Compose involves a comprehensive understanding of the lifecycle operations necessary to deploy, monitor, and update containerized applications effectively. This section elucidates the mechanisms and best practices for executing and administrating these applications, underscoring key Podman Compose commands and configurations pivotal for streamlined operations.

The cornerstone of multi-container management is effectively leveraging Podman Compose commands to control the application lifecycle. At its core, this process involves deploying instances, maintaining the active state, and updating the various elements of an application environment.

Starting Applications: To initiate multi-container applications defined within a Compose file, the up command is employed:

```
podman-compose up
```

Executing this command initiates all defined services in the foreground, with console output indicative of logs for troubleshooting purposes. The -d flag, when appended, enables detached execution, allowing the terminal to remain free for further use:

```
podman-compose up -d
```

Stopping Applications: Graceful termination of services is achieved with the down command, effectively stopping containers and removing associated networks.

```
podman-compose down
```

Efficient application management necessitates robust monitoring and logging to gain insight into runtime conditions and diagnose potential issues.

Service Logs: Accessing real-time logs from active services is facilitated through the logs command, which encapsulates output from containerized applications.

```
podman-compose logs
```

For streamlined analysis, specific service logs can be filtered by specifying the service name:

```
podman-compose logs servicename
```

Performance Monitoring: Podman's integration with traditional Linux tooling allows utilizing familiar monitoring tools such as `top`, `htop`, and `netstat` to observe container operations, resource usage, and network traffic.

The inherent horizontal scaling capabilities of containers enable administrators to modify the number of service instances as needed in response to dynamic workload requirements.

To scale a specified service, Podman Compose incorporates the `scale` command:

```
podman-compose up --scale web=3
```

This command increases the number of running `web` service containers to three, facilitating load distribution across instances.

Application evolution often necessitates configuration updates or software upgrades, tasks that Podman Compose facilitates via declarative changes in the Compose file followed by instance re-creation.

Environment Updates: Updating environment variables or configurations within a service definition requires editing the Compose file and applying changes through:

```
podman-compose up -d
```

This enactment reinitializes services with modified configurations, ensuring latest amendments take effect.

Rolling Updates: A strategy whereby services are updated incrementally to minimize downtime and maintain service continuity. Implementing rolling updates involves a combination of up and manual intervention to sequentially restart impacted services, often incorporating load balancers for traffic flow management.

Container networking flexibility within Podman Compose permits intricate network configurations that fit varying operational contexts.

Multi-Network Service Deployment: Services can operate on multiple networks concurrently, enabling complex routing and firewall strategies across internal and inter-service communications.

```
version: '3.7'

services:
  analytics:
    image: analytics:latest
    networks:
      - frontnet
      - backnet

networks:
  frontnet:
  backnet:
```

Network Policy Implementation: Podman Compose supports network policy scripting to limit intra-service communication, increasing security by controlling accessible pathways.

Navigating security constraints and ensuring robust containment involves taking precautions regarding container access controls, image security practices, and data protection.

Access Control: Rootless Podman enhances security by diminishing the risk from escalated permissions. Using Podman's uidmap options reinforces control over container privileges.

Image Verification: Routine image scanning ensures no vulnerabilities lie within downloaded images, augmented by secure storage of sensitive credentials through environment files:

```
version: '3.7'

services:
  db:
    image: postgres:latest
    env_file:
      - .env
```

Data persistence is central to long-lived application states and resilience against service termination.

```
version: '3.7'

services:
  stateful-service:
    image: app:latest
    volumes:
      - appdata:/var/lib/app

volumes:
  appdata:
```

By associating essential directories with volumes, data integrity sur-
vives through container cycles and re-orchestration.

Podman Compose empowers sysadmins and developers to harness an
organized approach to multi-container application execution, enhancing reliability via structured configuration management, operational
agility through powerful scaling, and architectural flexibility through
nuanced networking. Proficient execution of these practices, coupled
with vigilant resource stewardship and rigorous security, cultivates a
resilient and responsive container ecosystem.

8.5. Networking in Podman Compose

Networking is a pivotal component in the orchestration of multi-
container applications, enabling communication between containers,
services, and external networks. Podman Compose provides

sophisticated mechanisms to define and manage these network interactions, fostering seamless inter-container communication and robust network configurations. This section delves into the various networking types, configurations, and practices in Podman Compose, offering insights into optimizing container networks for efficient application deployment.

Understanding Podman Compose Networking Models

Podman Compose supports several network drivers, each serving distinct use-cases and operational scenarios. These fundamental principles guide the allocation and management of network resources within containerized environments.

1. Bridge Network: The default network mode when none is specified. Bridge networks serve as isolated networks for containers on the same host, allowing them to communicate with each other but maintaining isolation from external traffic.

```
version: '3.7'

services:
  service_a:
    image: nginx
  service_b:
    image: httpd
```

In this setup, service_a and service_b can communicate since they reside on the same default bridge network.

2. Host Network: In the host network mode, containers share the host's network stack, meaning there is no network isolation between the host and the container. This can provide performance gains by reducing network latency.

```
version: '3.7'

services:
  performance_critical_service:
    image: perf-opt-app
```

226

```
network_mode: host
```

This configuration is suitable for performance-sensitive applications where network isolation is not required and reduced network overhead is crucial.

3. None Network: This mode disables networking for the container, which can be useful for standalone applications that do not require any network interaction.

```
version: '3.7'

services:
  isolated_service:
    image: data-processor
    network_mode: none
```

4. Custom Bridge Networks: Custom bridge networks allow for dedicated network segments with distinct configurations, enhancing logical separation and control over container communications.

```
version: '3.7'

services:
  front:
    image: nginx
    networks:
      - frontend

  back:
    image: redis
    networks:
      - backend

networks:
  frontend:
    driver: bridge
  backend:
    driver: bridge
```

By specifying networks with custom drivers, services front and back are segregated into distinct network environments, amplifying security and reducing interference.

Inter-Service Communication and Network Configurations

Establishing clear and efficient communication channels between services is paramount for application consistency and performance within Podman Compose.

Service Discovery: Containers within the same network can access each other via service names, rendering explicit IP configuration unnecessary, thus simplifying configuration management.

```
version: '3.7'

services:
  app:
    image: node
    environment:
      - DATABASE_HOST=database

  database:
    image: postgres
```

Here, app connects to database using the environmental variable DATABASE_HOST, facilitating seamless internal connectivity through service names.

Aliases: Network aliases provide an alternative naming mechanism for services, enabling more flexible and readable network interactions.

```
version: '3.7'

services:
  cache:
    image: memcached
    networks:
      app_net:
        aliases:
          - cache.alias

networks:
  app_net:
```

The `cache` service is also accessible via the alias `cache.alias`, enhancing interoperability and compatibility in complex setups.

Connecting to External Networks

Containers frequently need access to external resources or integration with non-containerized services, achievable through explicit network configurations.

Exposing Ports: Port mappings bridge the external network traffic to internal container ports, paving the way for external interactions with container services.

```
version: '3.7'

services:
  web:
    image: mywebsite
    ports:
      - "80:8080"
```

In this example, traffic arriving at the host on port 80 is routed to port 8080 within the `web` container, facilitating external client access.

External Network Integration: Configurations often require linking Podman-managed networks with pre-existing external networks to route traffic through organization-wide infrastructures.

Security Considerations in Container Networking

Security remains a top priority within container networks, mandating configurations that secure container communications and inter-service interactions.

Network Isolation: Utilizing custom networks fortifies security by isolating services within defined network boundaries, obstructing unauthorized access pathways.

```
version: '3.7'

services:
```

229

```
secure_service:
  image: sensitive-app
  networks:
    - private_net

networks:
  private_net:
```

Encrypted Communications: Employing TLS/SSL within network traffic guarantees encrypted communications, ensuring data confidentiality and integrity between containers.

Firewall Configurations: Integrating Podman Compose with host-level firewall settings can control and restrict traffic at the network perimeter.

```
sudo firewall-cmd --add-port=8080/tcp --permanent
sudo firewall-cmd --reload
```

Network Troubleshooting and Diagnostics

To maintain an efficient network setup, administrators must have access to troubleshooting tools capable of diagnosing and resolving network issues in a containerized environment.

Inspecting Network Configurations: Podman CLI provides commands to inspect network states and configurations, presenting administrators with detailed insights into network functionalities.

```
podman network inspect
```

Analyzing Traffic: Using packet capturing tools such as Wireshark or tcpdump assists in visualizing traffic flow, identifying bottlenecks or anomalies in network performance.

Through leveraging Podman Compose's rich networking features, users can create reliable, scalable communication channels tailored to their architecture's needs. By understanding the available network modes, implementing best practices for secure and efficient communication, and utilizing robust diagnostic tools, a sophisticated and secure container network infrastructure can be achieved.

8.6. Scaling and Updating Services

The process of scaling and updating services in a Podman Compose environment underscores the flexibility and robustness of container-ized applications. Scaling services allows applications to handle vary-ing loads by adjusting the number of running instances, while updates ensure applications remain secure, reliable, and feature-rich. This sec-tion explores the methodologies, best practices, and technical consider-ations surrounding scaling and updating services in Podman Compose.

Horizontal Scaling of Services Horizontal scaling involves adjust-ing the number of container instances of a specific service. This flexibil-ity enables applications to respond dynamically to increased demand by spawning additional instances, thus distributing the load across multiple containers.

Implementing Scaling: Podman Compose simplifies the scaling process with the `scale` command, either set in the Compose file or ex-ecuted via the command line.

```
version: '3.7'

services:
  webapp:
    image: webapp:latest
    deploy:
      replicas: 3
```

In this setup, the webapp service initiates with three replicas, distribut-ing incoming requests across these instances for improved availability and responsiveness.

Dynamic Scaling: For runtime scaling adjustments, Podman Compose permits active manipulation of service instances.

```
podman-compose up --scale webapp=5
```

This command line directive expands the webapp instances to five, facilitating augmented capacity to handle load peaks without service interruption.

Load Balancing Strategies Properly scaling services often necessitates load balancing to distribute traffic effectively, thereby preventing bottlenecks and ensuring even workload distribution among replicas.

Internal Load Balancing: Podman Compose integrates with existing load balancing setups by configuring necessary port mappings and network aliases to abstract service endpoints.

Reverse Proxy Configuration: Employing reverse proxies like Nginx or HAProxy ensures efficient request routing and facilitates SSL termination, enhancing security and performance.

```
server {
    listen 80;

    location / {
        proxy_pass http://web-backend;
        proxy_set_header Host $host;
        proxy_set_header X-Real-IP $remote_addr;
    }
}

upstream web-backend {
    server webapp1:80;
    server webapp2:80;
    server webapp3:80;
}
```

In this Nginx configuration, traffic is balanced across three instances of webapp, effectively managing ingress traffic.

Handling Updates Gracefully Regular updates are crucial for maintaining the integrity and performance of services. Podman

Compose facilitates seamless updates through various strategies minimizing downtime and operational disruptions.

Rolling Updates: Implementing a rolling update strategy replaces container instances incrementally, maintaining service availability through the update process.

```
podman-compose up -d --no-deps myservice
```

This execution command updates myservice without stopping dependent services, orchestrating an orderly transition from old to new container versions.

Blue-Green Deployments: A Blue-Green deployment strategy sets up two parallel environments, redirecting traffic only when the new version is fully operational and tested.

```
version: '3.7'

services:
  website-blue:
    image: website:stable
    networks:
      - frontend

  website-green:
    image: website:latest
    networks:
      - frontend
```

In this configuration, traffic is manipulated between website-blue and website-green through DNS changes or reverse proxy configurations, facilitating safe version transitions.

Database Schema Migration Considerations Updates affecting the database schema require careful handling to prevent service disruptions and maintain data integrity.

Applying Migrations: Implement a strategy to apply database migrations alongside code updates without compromising availability.

```
podman-compose exec db bash -c "alembic upgrade head"
```

This command executes the Alembic database migration tool within the db service, updating the database schema in tandem with application changes.

Security Implications of Scaling and Updates Security remains a paramount concern during scaling and update operations. Ensuring container images are secure and the deployment pipeline encompasses proper security checks is essential.

Image Validation: Employ consistent image scanning procedures to detect vulnerabilities prior to deployment.

Access Control: Limit user permissions during deployment and runtime, ensuring only authorized personnel can execute updates or scaling commands.

Resource Management During Scaling Scaling must respect resource availability, requiring efficient allocation strategies that mitigate resource contention while maximizing performance:

- **CPU and Memory Allocation:** Ensure containers operate within defined resource constraints to prevent host system overload.

- **Network Bandwidth Utilization:** Balance bandwidth allocation to sustain quality service delivery during load transitions.

```
version: '3.7'

services:
  analytics:
    image: analytics:latest
    deploy:
      resources:
        limits:
          cpus: "2.0"
```

```
        memory: "2048M"
```

Operational Monitoring and Automation Smooth scaling and update processes rely heavily on real-time monitoring and automation tools:

Deploying Monitoring Solutions: Tools like Prometheus, ELK stack, or Grafana provide insights into application performance and operational health metrics.

```
version: '3.7'

services:
  prometheus:
    image: prom/prometheus
    ports:
      - "9090:9090"
    volumes:
      - ./prometheus.yml:/etc/prometheus/prometheus.yml
```

Automation Pipelines: Automate deployments using CI/CD pipelines to streamline scaling and updates while minimizing human error, integrating tests and build steps.

Best Practices for Scaling and Updating Conforming to best practices enhances efficiency, reduces risk, and ensures a seamless operational workflow:

- **Canary Releases:** Gradually roll out changes to a subset of users to validate new features before full-scale deployment.

- **Service Discovery Optimization:** Utilize service discovery tools for automated load distribution adjustments during scaling efforts.

- **Downtime Minimization:** Implement zero-downtime strategies like Blue-Green deployments and test changes in staging environments prior to production rollout.

By understanding and employing these techniques, administrators and developers create a dynamic, scalable, and adaptable application architecture capable of meeting evolving business and technical demands, all while maintaining secure and efficient operations.

Chapter 9

Security Best Practices with Podman

This chapter emphasizes securing containerized environments with Podman by utilizing rootless mode to minimize privilege-related risks. It discusses methods for safeguarding container images through scanning, signing, and using trusted sources. Networking security is addressed by implementing firewalls and policies. The chapter provides insights into using Podman's security features, such as capabilities and seccomp profiles, to enforce robust security policies. Additionally, it highlights the importance of monitoring and auditing container activities to prevent and respond to security incidents, ensuring a secure and resilient operational environment.

9.1. Fundamentals of Container Security

Container security is an emerging discipline focused on the protections and defenses applied to containerized applications and environments. Being at the forefront of modern DevOps practices, containers bring unique security advantages and challenges. As you delve into the essentials of securing containerized applications, understanding these foundational elements is imperative.

The core of container security lies in addressing both the intrinsic characteristics of containers and the infrastructure that supports them. Containers offer a degree of isolation between processes, yet they share the same operating system kernel. This inherent sharing poses security risks distinct from traditional virtual machines.

Namespace Isolation

Namespaces are the building blocks of container isolation. They provide the illusion that a process has its private view of the operating system, which includes process IDs (PIDs), file system, user IDs (UIDs), network stacks, and more. It's vital to ensure these namespaces are properly configured to protect the container from unauthorized interactions.

For example, PID namespaces isolate the process ID number space, meaning that process IDs inside the namespace can be identical to process IDs outside without conflict or interaction. This isolation is shown in the following example:

```
# Create a new PID namespace
$ unshare --pid --fork /bin/bash

# Inside this new namespace
$ echo $$  # Shows the shell's PID in the new namespace
1

# Outside the namespace
$ echo $$  # Shows the original shell's PID
```

238

```
1234
```

This example illustrates that the isolated shell believes it is the root process PID 1 within the namespace, exemplifying isolation.

Control Groups (cgroups)

Control groups limit, account for, and isolate the CPU, memory, disk I/O, and networking resources used by containerized applications. By enforcing limits, cgroups prevent a container from using excessive resources, which helps maintain the overall system's stability and security.

```
# Limiting CPU usage with cgroups
$ cgcreate -g cpu:/restricted

# Set CPU share to 512 (out of 1024)
$ cgset -r cpu.shares=512 /restricted

# Run a command under these constraints
$ cgexec -g cpu:restricted mycontainer
```

This approach effectively restricts the container labeled mycontainer to half of the CPU resource in the context of the system's total available resources, enhancing fairness and security.

Capabilities

Linux capabilities break down the all-encompassing root privileges into distinct units. Containers can be granted only the capabilities they require, reducing the damage potential in case of a breach.

To illustrate, consider the NET_BIND_SERVICE capability, which is the capability to bind a socket to privileged ports (those below 1024). A container needing to bind to port 80 could be granted just this capability without full root privileges:

```
# Drop all capabilities and add just NET_BIND_SERVICE
$ docker run --cap-drop ALL --cap-add NET_BIND_SERVICE mywebapp
```

Here, by dropping all unnecessary capabilities and adding only the essential NET_BIND_SERVICE, the container is hardened against elevation-of-privilege exploits.

Seccomp Profiles

Seccomp (secure computing mode) restricts the set of system calls that applications can make. Since containers should use only a limited number of system calls in practice, defining strict seccomp profiles can significantly mitigate risks associated with malicious or flawed applications.

```
{
  "defaultAction": "SCMP_ACT_ERRNO",
  "syscalls": [
    {
      "names": [
        "getcwd",
        "write",
        "read"
      ],
      "action": "SCMP_ACT_ALLOW"
    }
  ]
}
```

In this JSON seccomp profile example, the container is allowed only to execute 'getcwd', 'write', and 'read'. Any other system calls would fail with a permission error, preventing potential misuse.

Image Integrity

Images form the core code base of containers, thus they must be secure and trusted. Employing techniques such as image signing and scanning helps ensure integrity and authenticity. Signing images involves using cryptographic keys to verify the source and authenticity of a container image.

Image scanning identifies vulnerabilities in base images before they reach production. This process detects known vulnerabilities and ensures compliance with organizational policies.

```
# Inspect an image for vulnerabilities using a tool like Trivy
$ trivy image mycontainer:latest
```

Executing this type of analysis helps identify potential risks and patch them prior to deployment.

Kubernetes Network Policies

Within orchestrated environments like Kubernetes, network policies serve as the primary way to control communication flows between pods. Properly defining network policies can prevent unauthorized communication, reduce lateral movement, and contain possible breaches.

A typical network policy in Kubernetes might resemble:

```
apiVersion: networking.k8s.io/v1
kind: NetworkPolicy
metadata:
  name: deny-all
  namespace: default
spec:
  podSelector: {}
  policyTypes:
  - Egress
  - Ingress
  ingress: []
  egress: []
```

The above policy explicitly denies all ingress and egress traffic to and from all pods within the 'default' namespace unless otherwise specified.

Security Contexts in Kubernetes

Security contexts define privilege and access levels for pods or containers, ensuring secure execution environments. Key settings include user and group IDs, privilege escalation prevention, and read-only file system enforcement.

```
apiVersion: v1
kind: Pod
metadata:
  name: secure-pod
spec:
  containers:
  - name: secure-container
    image: myimage
    securityContext:
      runAsUser: 1000
      readOnlyRootFilesystem: true
      allowPrivilegeEscalation: false
```

In this configuration, the 'secure-container' runs under a non-root user (ID 1000), uses a read-only root filesystem, and blocks privilege escalation, fortifying the container's operational security.

With these fundamental principles, securing containerized applications involves a meticulous process of understanding and implementing isolation, access control, resource management, and proactive defense mechanisms. Attention to these core aspects of container security is essential for building resilient and trustworthy containerized environments.

9.2. Running Containers in Rootless Mode

Running containers in rootless mode is an advanced technique to enhance security by executing containers without root privileges. This approach mitigates the risks associated with running containers that might be exploited to gain unauthorized access to the host system. By refraining from invoking root-level permissions, rootless containers provide an additional security layer, preventing an attacker from escalating privileges if a container is compromised.

Rootless mode leverages the unique capabilities of user namespaces in the Linux kernel. User namespaces enable the mapping of user IDs

(UIDs) from within the container to a different set on the host system, effectively allowing processes to assume root inside the container while being a regular user on the host. This separation of user identity is foundational for running containers safely without superuser privileges on the host.

User Namespaces and UID Mapping

The core concept behind rootless containers is the manipulation of user namespaces. A user namespace allows processes to have their own independent set and mappings of user and group IDs. This capability enables the mapping of the root user inside a container to a non-root UID on the host, enhancing security by isolating potentially harmful processes.

Consider the command:

```
unshare --user --map-root-user bash
```

Executing this command inside the rootless container environment allows a shell session to start with the root UID mapped to a non-privileged UID on the host, shown by:

```
id -u
0

echo $$
1001
```

Although the user appears as root (with 'id -u' returning 0) within the namespace, they correspond to UID 1001 on the host system ('echo $$' representing a non-privileged process).

Rootless Container Engines: Podman

Podman is a container engine designed to comply with the rootless paradigm, allowing users to execute containers without the daemon privileges needed in some traditional container environments like

Docker. By design, Podman can run containers in a manner similar to running processes directly, with command-line interfaces offering nearly identical functionality to Docker but without the need for elevated privileges on the host.

Starting a rootless container with Podman is straightforward:

```
podman run --rm -it nginx
```

Internally, Podman automatically configures the necessary user namespaces and maps the container's UIDs to ensure isolation from host processes.

Network Configuration in Rootless Mode

Networking in rootless containers presents a unique challenge, as containers do not hold privileged access to manipulate network configurations directly. Podman addresses this by integrating with network namespaces and leveraging a user-level network stack to provide virtual Ethernet devices.

Packet forwarding and port mapping function differently due to these restrictions, often requiring additional setups such as fisheries with TUN/TAP devices or VPN-based configurations. However, Podman seamlessly abstracts this complexity, offering network functionalities akin to privileged containers.

```
podman run --rm -p 8080:80 nginx
```

Despite the constraints, Podman enables port forwarding, opening the container's port 80 to communication through host port 8080, thanks to rootless tunneling features.

Filesystem Isolation and Volumes

Rootless containers mirror the host filesystem environment via user namespaces and Control Groups (cgroups). When mounting volumes, it's crucial to understand how UID mappings affect file access. If a host directory is mounted into a container, the UID mappings will determine the permissions and accessibility.

For instance:

```
podman run --rm -v /home/user/data:/data nginx
```

Inside the container, '/data' could be owned by user root (UID 0) when referenced by container processes. However, these files map to user 1000 on the host, ensuring malicious container processes cannot leverage root capabilities to alter host data.

Security Considerations

Deploying rootless containers reinforces security by drastically reducing the attack surface inherent in privileged containers. This reduction is primarily due to limited access to system files and the inability to modify kernel settings or network interfaces without appropriate privileges, maintaining a stance akin to principles of least privilege.

The reduced privileges come with trade-offs, notably a lack of access to certain kernel resources, constraints in directly accessing network interfaces, and restricted filesystem capabilities. Nevertheless, for many applications, these limitations are acceptable given the security benefits obtained.

Utilizing Rootless Mode in Kubernetes

In clustered environments such as Kubernetes, rootless containers provide a measure of security at the pod level. Kubernetes does not inherently operate using rootless containers, but it can be configured to deploy containers with minimized privileges fitting within user namespaces, often integrating network policies and Pod Security Policies (PSPs) to ensure rootless compliance.

A basic configuration might enforce non-root user execution with:

```
apiVersion: v1
kind: Pod
metadata:
  name: rootless-pod
spec:
  securityContext:
    runAsUser: 1000
  containers:
  - name: rootless-container
    image: nginx
    securityContext:
      runAsNonRoot: true
      allowPrivilegeEscalation: false
```

This configuration effectively defines a pod running in a safer configuration by using a user namespace, avoiding elevation permissions and ensuring container processes adhere to security policies.

Advanced Use Cases

Rootless mode's design shines within environments requiring multitenancy where several users run containers simultaneously on shared hosts. Advanced deployments can automate UID/GID map allocation and reconciliation, ensuring process isolation both among containers and with respect to the host environment.

Rootless containers also thrive in Developer Environments, providing safe, controlled access without administrative privileges, often through composable tools like podman-compose, which mirrors Docker Compose functionality while leveraging Podman's rootless capabilities.

The journey to rootless environs remains in active development, gaining maturity with advancements in kernel features, tooling improvements, and comprehensive community input. This progression positions rootless operations as a cornerstone for secure, scalable, and efficient container implementations.

9.3. Securing Container Images

Container images form the fundamental building block of container-ized applications. Their integrity and security are critical as they encapsulate the application code, its dependencies, and configuration files. A compromised image can lead to widespread vulnerabilities, potentially exposing systems to attacks. Therefore, securing container images is a vital component of the container security lifecycle, involving processes such as image creation, scanning for vulnerabilities, signing, and using trusted registries.

Image Creation Best Practices

The process of creating secure images starts with the base image selection. Choosing minimal and official base images decreases the attack surface and the number of vulnerabilities. Minimal base images like alpine offer reduced sizes and components, lowering the risk profile.

```
# Use a minimal base image to reduce vulnerabilities
FROM alpine:latest

# Install only necessary packages
RUN apk add --no-cache nginx

# Copy application code
COPY . /app

# Set the entrypoint
ENTRYPOINT ["nginx", "-g", "daemon off;"]
```

In this example, employing alpine:latest as a base image ensures the image remains simple and free of unnecessary components.

Additionally, during image creation, applying multistage builds can enhance security. Multistage builds separate the build environment from the final runtime, ensuring only the minimum required files are included in the final image.

```
# Builder stage
```

```
FROM golang:1.16 as builder
WORKDIR /app
COPY . .
RUN go build -o myapp

# Final stage
FROM alpine:latest
WORKDIR /app
COPY --from=builder /app/myapp .
ENTRYPOINT ["./myapp"]
```

In this setup, the Go application is built in a separate stage, reducing the final image size and eliminating unnecessary build tools, promoting a secure deployment.

Image Vulnerability Scanning

Scanning container images for vulnerabilities preemptively identifies security issues before they impact production systems. Tools such as Trivy, Clair, and Anchore evaluate images against known vulnerabilities databases (NVD) to provide actionable insights about present risks.

Here's an example utilizing Trivy to scan an image for vulnerabilities:

```
# Scan an image for vulnerabilities
$ trivy image nginx:latest
```

The output provides a detailed report of vulnerabilities identified within the image, categorized by severity, enabling developers to address critical issues swiftly.

Library	Vulnerability ID	Severity	Installed Version	Fixed Version	Title
libapk3	CVE-2021-36159	HIGH	2.12.5-r0	2.12.6-r0	libapk3: Heap out-of-bounds read in apk_cache_download in apk_fetch_instance()

Address vulnerabilities either by updating packages to non-vulnerable versions or replacing dependencies. Integrating routine scans within a Continuous Integration/Continuous Deployment (CI/CD) pipeline ensures persistent monitoring and alerts stakeholders to new vulnerabilities.

Image Signing and Verification

Digital signatures confirm the origin and integrity of container images. By signing images, developers attest to their authenticity, allowing consumers to verify they are using the intended versions without tampering.

An effective signing workflow could use tools like Docker Content Trust or Sigstore:

```
# Enable Docker Content Trust
$ export DOCKER_CONTENT_TRUST=1

# Sign and push an image
$ docker push myregistry.com/myimage:latest
```

Once an image is signed, it's crucial to verify its signature during deployment to ensure the image integrity has not been compromised:

```
# Pull an image with verification
$ docker pull myregistry.com/myimage:latest
```

Here, Docker automatically checks the image signature, refusing to pull unsigned images when Docker Content Trust is enabled, thus securing the deployment pipeline.

Using Trusted Registries

The deployment of images from trusted registries assists in establishing a reliable source of container images. Trusted registries like Docker Hub, Google Container Registry (GCR), and Amazon Elastic Container Registry (ECR) enforce security controls by scanning and verifying images for vulnerabilities, offering users peace of mind regarding image provenance.

Employing private registries also affords organizations more control over access and auditability, enabling enforcement of stricter security policies and integration with internal authentication systems.

```
# Pulling from a private registry
$ docker login myprivateregistry.com
$ docker pull myprivateregistry.com/myapp:latest
```

By credential-guarding access to a private registry, sensitive images are shielded from unauthorized entities, minimizing the risk of exposure or exploitation.

Ongoing Image Management and Policies

Sustained security necessitates continuous image management, involving routine updates and comprehensive policies. Policies should define base image update cadences, supported image lifetimes, and deprecation timelines for vulnerable images.

Automated scripts or tools can facilitate updating base images to patched versions, aligning them with established organizational policies. Here's an example of a simple script for automating image updates:

```
#!/bin/bash

# Pull the latest base image
docker pull alpine:latest

# Rebuild application images
docker build -t myapp:latest .

# Redeploy updated images
docker service update --image myapp:latest myservice
```

A combination of vigilant management and enforcement through Infrastructure as Code (IaC) or policy frameworks supports ongoing image integrity.

Integrating Security into the Development Lifecycle

Security must be integrated into the entire development lifecycle to ensure comprehensive protection. Initiatives such as DevSecOps harmonize development, security, and operations, embedding security practices directly into workflows.

By incorporating image security checks at multiple stages—from development and staging to production—developers can preempt weaknesses and instate controls proactively rather than reactively. Language-specific linters, static analysis tools, and automated testing augment these checks by ensuring code contributions don't inadvertently introduce vulnerabilities.

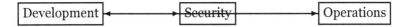

In the DevSecOps loop, security considerations guide development strategies just as operational constraints influence decisions, forging a reliable container image security framework.

Emerging Trends and Solutions

As containerization expands, advancements in container image security tech continue to blossom. Solutions like BuildKit and Kaniko optimize secure image building, while Open Policy Agent (OPA) opens new frontiers in policy-driven security, dynamically verifying policy compliance within the CD pipeline.

Aspects of Machine Learning (ML) and Artificial Intelligence (AI) have also begun entering the arena. These technologies can analyze patterns in image data, identifying potential threats that escape traditional detection.

By fostering a security-focused culture, continuously training teams about emerging threats, and proactively adopting novel strategies, organizations remain poised to tackle evolving challenges related to container image security.

9.4. Implementing Network Security for Containers

Network security is a critical facet of securing containerized applications, as containers communicate across distributed and dynamic environments. Implementing robust network security measures for containers involves comprehensive strategies, from controlling ingress and egress traffic to enabling secure communication between containers and external entities.

The dynamic nature of container environments necessitates flexibility and adaptability in network security. Container orchestration tools like Kubernetes provide built-in systems to manage network security in a scalable fashion. Nevertheless, this domain requires a profound understanding of network configurations, policy implementations, and security considerations specific to containerized applications.

Network Namespaces and Virtual Interfaces

Containers utilize network namespaces to isolate their networking stacks. Each container can have its own network devices, IP addresses, routing tables, and /etc/resolv.conf, all isolated from others. This segregation is achieved using virtual interfaces mapped across namespace boundaries to facilitate communication with other containers and the host.

```
# Create a new network namespace
$ ip netns add container-ns

# Create a virtual Ethernet pair (veth)
$ ip link add veth0 type veth peer name veth1

# Move one end of the veth to the container network namespace
$ ip link set veth1 netns container-ns

# Assign IP addresses
$ ip addr add 192.168.0.1/24 dev veth0
$ ip netns exec container-ns ip addr add 192.168.0.2/24 dev veth1
```

```
# Bring interfaces up
$ ip link set dev veth0 up
$ ip netns exec container-ns ip link set dev veth1 up
```

This example demonstrates establishing a separate network namespace for container isolation with a virtual Ethernet pair bridging connectivity.

Network Security Policies

Kubernetes Network Policies allow operators to define how pods within a Kubernetes cluster are allowed to communicate with each other and network endpoints. Leveraging network policies provides granular controls over traffic flow, helping to minimize undesired access and reinforce cluster security.

Here's a typical network policy enforcing strict controls:

```
apiVersion: networking.k8s.io/v1
kind: NetworkPolicy
metadata:
  name: allow-nginx-ingress
  namespace: mynamespace
spec:
  podSelector:
    matchLabels:
      app: nginx
  policyTypes:
  - Ingress
  ingress:
  - from:
    - podSelector:
        matchLabels:
          role: frontend
    ports:
    - protocol: TCP
      port: 80
```

In this policy, only pods labeled frontend are permitted to ingress traffic to pods running nginx on port 80. Policies like these reduce unauthorized access by explicitly defining allowed interactions within the network.

Service Mesh Implementations

A service mesh facilitates observability, security, and control over
service-to-service communications within container environments. By
abstracting complex networking logic out of applications and delegat-
ing it to a mesh layer, operators gain significant flexibility in managing
and enforcing networking policies.

Service meshes like Istio offer robust features including mutual TLS
(mTLS), allowing encrypted traffic between services without altering
application logic:

```
# Enable mTLS for a namespace using Istio
kubectl label namespace mynamespace istio-injection=enabled

# Apply a PeerAuthentication policy
kubectl apply -f - <<EOF
apiVersion: security.istio.io/v1beta1
kind: PeerAuthentication
metadata:
  name: default
  namespace: mynamespace
spec:
  mtls:
    mode: STRICT
EOF
```

Here, mTLS is enforced for all services within 'mynamespace', ensuring data privacy and authentication for intra-service communications.

Firewall Implementations

Implementing firewalls at both the host and network levels fortifies
container network security. Host-based firewalls using tools like iptables or nftables define rules to control packet processing within and
between containers.

```
# Deny all inbound traffic to a specific container
$ iptables -A INPUT -s 0.0.0.0/0 -d 192.168.1.10 -j DROP
```

```
# Allow specific inbound traffic over port 80
$ iptables -A INPUT -s 0.0.0.0/0 -d 192.168.1.10 --dport 80 -j ACCEPT
```

Through these commands, iptables drop incoming traffic by default and only permit connections to a container on port 80, reducing exposure to only necessary services.

Ingress Controllers and Load Balancers

Ingress controllers manage external traffic entering a Kubernetes cluster, routing it to the appropriate services. They balance the traffic load, ensuring application reliability and security. By integrating with external certificates and authorization mechanisms, ingress controllers offer SSL/TLS termination capabilities that enhance secure access to applications.

```
apiVersion: networking.k8s.io/v1
kind: Ingress
metadata:
  name: example-ingress
  namespace: mynamespace
annotations:
  nginx.ingress.kubernetes.io/ssl-redirect: "true"
spec:
  rules:
  - host: example.com
    http:
      paths:
      - path: /
        pathType: Prefix
        backend:
          service:
            name: myservice
            port:
              number: 80
  tls:
  - hosts:
    - example.com
    secretName: example-tls
```

This ingress rule applies SSL/TLS to traffic destined for 'example.com', ensuring secure client-server communication by redirecting nonsecure HTTP traffic to HTTPS.

DNS Security Practices

Secure Domain Name System (DNS) configurations are essential within container environments to prevent DNS spoofing and cache poisoning attacks. By operating internal DNS services and applying strict DNS policies, containers rely on authoritative and trusted data for network operations.

```
# Example of setting up a CoreDNS entry
kubectl apply -f - <<EOF
apiVersion: v1
kind: ConfigMap
metadata:
  name: coredns-custom
  namespace: kube-system
data:
  example.server: |
    example.local:53 {
      forward . /etc/resolv.conf
    }
EOF
```

The configuration ensures DNS queries for 'example.local' are directed through recognized channels, providing a secure resolution path within the cluster.

Container Network Interface (CNI) Plugins

CNI plugins provide a consistent interface for configuring network interfaces within Linux containers. They play a core role in Kubernetes to manage network connectivity. Leveraging plugins such as Calico or Weave can enforce network security through advanced policy definitions and network segmentation.

Calico, for instance, provides a robust network security framework with capabilities for enforcing policies on both layer 3 and layer 7 data:

```
apiVersion: crd.projectcalico.org/v1
kind: NetworkPolicy
metadata:
```

```
  name: allow-tcp-80
  namespace: mynamespace
spec:
  selector: role == 'frontend'
  ingress:
  - action: Allow
    protocol: TCP
    destination:
      ports:
      - 80
```

This policy specifically allows TCP traffic to frontend roles on port 80, structured for advanced control over network access.

Best Practices and Ongoing Management

Implementing comprehensive network security strategies requires best practices rooted in least privilege, zero-trust frameworks, and real-time monitoring. Detailed logging facilitates vigilance over network activities, enabling the swift detection and mitigation of potentially malicious actions.

Employing tools such as Grafana, Prometheus, and ELK (Elasticsearch, Logstash, Kibana) stacks enables customizable metric collection and visualization, supporting continuous network security enhancements:

```
# Run a Prometheus & Grafana monitoring setup
docker run -d --name=grafana -p 3000:3000 grafana/grafana
docker run -d --name=prometheus -p 9090:9090 prom/prometheus
```

Strong user authentication and maintaining up-to-date security certificates are also vital, guaranteeing that only authorized users access sensitive networked services.

Security is an iterative process, where continuous evaluation and adaptation allow for alignment with evolving threats. Leveraging container logs, responding to security audits, and enforcing regular penetration testing fortify a containerized network environment against an ever-changing threat landscape.

257

9.5. Using Podman for Enforcing Security Policies

Podman is a container management tool that distinguishes itself by running without a central daemon, offering enhanced security and flexibility for enforcing security policies across containerized environments. Its ability to execute containers in a rootless mode and integrate seamlessly into existing Linux authentication systems provides significant advantages in maintaining robust security postures. This section delves into the ways Podman can be employed to enforce comprehensive security policies effectively.

Rootless Operation and User Namespaces

Podman's rootless mode is pivotal to its security framework. By utilizing user namespaces, Podman maps the container user's privileges to those of a non-privileged user on the host, greatly reducing the risk of privilege escalation exploits.

Consider the following command to run a container in rootless mode:

```
$ podman run --rm -d nginx
```

Internally, Podman configures user namespace maps so that container operations perceive themselves running as root, while on the host, they operate with standard user permissions. This configuration narrows the attack surface and protects host integrity even if a container is compromised.

Capability Management with Podman

Linux capabilities offer fine-grained control over privileged operations, allowing users to assign only necessary permissions to containers. Podman supports managing capabilities, enabling tailored permissions to minimize potential security risks:

```
# Run a Podman container with limited capabilities
$ podman run --rm --cap-drop=ALL --cap-add=NET_BIND_SERVICE nginx
```

This command revokes all capabilities except `NET_BIND_SERVICE`, which allows the container to bind to network ports below 1024, providing a necessary privilege without broader entitlements that could be abused.

Seccomp Security Profiles

Using seccomp profiles, Podman can restrict the system calls containers can invoke, mitigating the risk of kernel-level exploits. Default seccomp policies deny calls that aren't strictly necessary, aligning with the principle of least privilege:

```
{
  "defaultAction": "SCMP_ACT_ERRNO",
  "syscalls": [
    {
      "names": [
        "write",
        "read",
        "close"
      ],
      "action": "SCMP_ACT_ALLOW"
    }
  ]
}
```

This reduced syscall set minimizes the container's ability to influence system operations, forming a robust barrier against low-level attacks.

Managing Container IDs and Groups

Utilizing user and group identifications (UIDs and GIDs) is another crucial aspect of Podman's security capabilities. By managing mappings securely, you ensure that container operations adhere to host policies:

```
# Create a new Podman container with a specific UID/GID
$ podman run --rm -u 1001:1001 nginx
```

Running containers with specific UIDs/GIDs limits their ability to interact with restricted files and processes, providing an additional layer of protection through compartmentalization.

Networking and Firewall Rules

Network policies controlled at the Podman level enhance security by managing inter-container communication and external access. Firewall rules can be tailored using `iptables` to enforce rigorously controlled network traffic adherence:

```
# Allow Podman container to communicate only with specific IP ranges
$ iptables -A OUTPUT -o eth0 -p tcp -m multiport --sports 8080 -d
    192.168.1.0/24 -j ACCEPT
$ iptables -A OUTPUT -o eth0 -p tcp -m multiport --sports 8080 -j
    DROP
```

These rules ensure that network access from within a container, specifically on port 8080, adheres to predetermined security policies, crucial in controlling lateral movement within a broader containerized system.

Podman Volume Security and Access Controls

Volumes in Podman facilitate persistent storage but necessitate stringent access controls. Ensuring appropriate file system permissions and using Podman's volume capabilities mitigates unauthorized data access:

```
# Securely mount a volume with specific permissions
$ podman run --rm -v /srv/data:/data:ro nginx
```

This command mounts the host directory at `/srv/data` into the container in a read-only mode, safeguarding sensitive data from unauthorized write operations potentially emanating from within the container.

Podman Pods and Isolation

Podman's concept of pods extends the paradigm of process grouping, enhancing security by isolating collections of containers using shared networking and storage settings. This setup allows enforcement of consistent policies across logically grouped containers.

```
# Create a Podman pod to group containers
$ podman pod create --name mypod

# Run containers within this pod
$ podman run --pod=mypod -d nginx
$ podman run --pod=mypod -d redis
```

Organizing containers into pods enables shared security configurations, such as network namespaces, thereby simplifying the application of uniform security policies across diverse services.

Automated Policy Enforcement and Auditing

Automation is key to maintaining effective security governance. By leveraging Podman in conjunction with CI/CD pipelines, automated security checks can be rigorously enforced:

```
# Scan Podman image using Trivy prior to deployment
$ trivy image mypodmanimage:latest
```

Ensuring containers pass security scans before integration into production pipelines helps maintain continuous vigilance against vulnerabilities. Logs and audit trails generated by Podman facilitate ongoing monitoring and forensic analysis, supporting compliance with industry standards and regulations.

DevSecOps Integration and Secure Development Practices

Podman supports integrating security seamlessly into DevOps practices, transitioning to a DevSecOps model where security becomes an intrinsic part of the development lifecycle. With Podman's interoperability with existing development tools, embedding security policies directly into deployment scripts and container definitions is straightforward:

```
# Incorporate Podman into CI pipeline, ensuring secure deployment
```

```
$ podman build -t secureimage .
$ podman run --rm --name=test -d secureimage && podman test-container
    test
```

This integration enforces a security-first approach not as an afterthought but as a critical component of the deployment cycle.

Compliance and Regulatory Adherence

Podman also assists organizations in attaining and maintaining compliance with stringent regulations like PCI-DSS, HIPAA, and GDPR. Through detailed logging capabilities and audit trails, Podman delivers transparency and accountability that bolster compliance efforts.

Logs generated during container operations, accessible through Podman's CLI commands, form critical evidence for auditor review, validating compliance with data protection standards.

As threats evolve, Podman's commitment to incorporating the latest in security best practices makes it an ideal tool for enforcing robust security policies in containerized environments. By leveraging its capabilities, coupled with enterprise frameworks and regulatory compliance requirements, organizations can build secure, scalable, and compliant container deployments.

9.6.   Monitoring and Auditing Container Activity

Effective monitoring and auditing of container activity is crucial for maintaining security and operational integrity in containerized environments. As containers facilitate rapid application deployment, understanding their behavior through monitoring can provide early indications of potential security incidents, system failures, or performance bottlenecks. Additionally, auditing provides a historical record of actions for compliance and forensic investigations. This section explores the comprehensive mechanisms for monitoring and auditing container activity, with practical insights and examples.

Understanding Container Monitoring

Container monitoring involves tracking various metrics and events to evaluate the performance, availability, and integrity of containerized applications. Key metrics include CPU and memory utilization, disk I/O, network traffic, and application-specific measures, such as request rates or error frequencies. By collecting these metrics, teams can gain insights into container behavior, optimizing resource usage and promptly addressing issues.

A commonly utilized tool for this purpose is Prometheus, a powerful open-source monitoring system:

```
# Sample Prometheus configuration to scrape metrics from containers
scrape_configs:
  - job_name: 'containers'
    static_configs:
      - targets: ['localhost:9090']
```

In this example, Prometheus is configured to scrape metrics from containers, allowing for detailed tracking and analysis of resource usage and application performance.

Comprehensive Logging Solutions

Logging is an integral part of monitoring, providing context and visibility into the operations of containers. Logs capture detailed records of activities, such as application logs, system events, and access logs, which are critical for diagnosing issues and understanding system states.

Docker and Podman natively support logging drivers to streamline log collection:

```
# Run a container with JSON logging driver
$ docker run --log-driver=json-file nginx
```

263

```
# Access container logs
$ docker logs <container_id>
```

Log drivers like `json-file` enable log output to be stored in JSON format, facilitating easier parsing and integration with centralized logging solutions. Containers can also be configured to use platforms like Fluentd or the ELK (Elasticsearch, Logstash, Kibana) stack for aggregation and analysis.

```
# Configure Docker to use Fluentd log driver
$ vim /etc/docker/daemon.json
{
  "log-driver": "fluentd",
  "log-opts": {
    "fluentd-address": "localhost:24224"
  }
}
```

This configuration highlights how containers can forward logs to a centralized Fluentd instance, easing administration by consolidating log management.

Real-Time Monitoring and Alerts

Beyond simple log collection, real-time monitoring capabilities allow teams to respond quickly to potential issues or attacks. Implementing alert systems ensures timely notifications based on defined thresholds or anomalous patterns. Systems like Grafana, integrated with Prometheus or Loki for logs, provide dashboards and alerting capabilities.

```
# Configure Grafana to send alerts based on Prometheus data
curl -X POST -H "Content-Type: application/json" \
-d '{
  "name": "High CPU Usage",
  "condition": "avg() > 70",
  "evaluationInterval": "1m",
  "sendNotification": true
}' http://localhost:3000/api/alerts
```

Alerts configured like this example enable administration teams to receive notifications when CPU usage surpasses 70% for a sustained period, aiding in proactive resource management.

Security Auditing

Auditing involves systematically recording activities to ensure compliance, facilitate forensic analysis, and verify system integrity. A rigorous audit trail captures user actions, system changes, and security-sensitive operations within container environments. Native command logging, security frameworks like Open Policy Agent (OPA), and layer-specific auditing (e.g., Kubernetes audit logging) assist in this effort.

```
# Sample Kubernetes audit policy
apiVersion: audit.k8s.io/v1
kind: Policy
rules:
  - level: Metadata
    resources:
      - group: ""
        resources: ["pods", "secrets"]
```

This Kubernetes audit policy records requests for pods and secrets at the metadata level, keeping detailed logs for compliance checks or investigations.

Enhancing Visibility with Network Analysis

Network monitoring solutions within containers, such as Cilium or Calico, supplement audit logs by providing granular views into network traffic. These solutions offer policy enforcement and observability at the network layer.

Cilium, for instance, supports the inspection of container communication with additional metrics and comprehensive HTTP request logs:

```
# Install Cilium for network observability
$ cilium install

# Analyze HTTP requests
$ cilium monitor --http
```

Implementing a solution like Cilium helps track inter-container communication, enhancing the security posture against unauthorized access or data exfiltration.

Container Security Platforms and Integrations

Comprehensive security platforms like Aqua Security, Sysdig Secure, and Twistlock facilitate container monitoring and auditing through advanced integrations:

- **Aqua Security** provides vulnerability scanning, access controls, and runtime protection.

- **Sysdig Secure** specializes in runtime threat detection, leveraging syscall-based monitoring.

- **Twistlock** offers image scanning, compliance management, and application-layer networking security.

These platforms integrate with container orchestration systems to provide end-to-end security, monitoring, and compliance management, reducing the complexity of securing numerous containers at scale.

CI/CD Pipeline Integration

The integration of monitoring and auditing tools within CI/CD pipelines ensures continuous security checks from development to production. By incorporating monitoring scripts, testing harnesses, and automated analysis tools, organizations can detect and resolve vulnerabilities earlier in the development lifecycle.

```
# Example pipeline with Jenkins
pipeline {
  agent any
  stages {
    stage('Build') {
```

```
    steps {
      script {
        sh 'docker build -t myapp .'
      }
    }
  }
  stage('Test') {
    steps {
      script {
        sh 'docker run myapp:latest test'
      }
    }
  }
  stage('Security Check') {
    steps {
      script {
        sh 'trivy image myapp:latest'
      }
    }
  }
}
}
```

This Jenkins pipeline demonstrates the deployment of secure practices by introducing mandatory security checks during the build process, with automated vulnerability scans and results analysis before proceeding to production.

Implementing Best Practices in Monitoring and Auditing

Achieving a comprehensive strategy for container monitoring and auditing involves adhering to best practices:

- **Standardization**: Develop standard logging formats and levels to facilitate consistent data interpretation and aggregation.

- **Optimization**: Optimize monitoring and logging scale to balance detailed data collection with performance considerations.

- **Regular Audits**: Conduct regular security audits to mitigate risks and ensure cross-organizational compliance.

- **Incident Response Planning**: Ensure comprehensive incident response plans incorporating monitoring data to accelerate resolution workflows.

- **Continuous Improvement**: Iterate and adapt monitoring strategies based on evolving threats and insights gained from historical data review.

The integration of monitoring and auditing mechanisms into the container lifecycle helps establish observability, identify and address security vulnerabilities, and guarantee compliance. By leveraging a combination of toolsets, organizations can build powerful systems that proactively secure container environments, ensuring resilient application deployments.

Chapter 10

Troubleshooting and Optimizing Container Performance in Podman

This chapter provides strategies for diagnosing common container issues using Podman's tools and techniques. It emphasizes the importance of logs for effective troubleshooting and guides on optimizing resource usage to enhance container performance. Techniques for reducing image size and improving loading speeds are discussed, alongside strategies for optimizing network performance for containers. The chapter concludes with methods for monitoring and tuning Podman configurations to achieve consistent and optimal operational efficiency, equipping users with comprehensive

skills for maintaining high performance in containerized applications.

10.1. Diagnosing Common Container Issues

In containerized applications, the proper functioning and utilization of containers are paramount. Containers encapsulate an application and its dependencies in a lightweight, portable package, thereby simplifying deployment across different environments. However, this abstraction layer can obscure the visibility of underlying issues that may arise. Understanding how to diagnose such problems effectively is a critical skill in ensuring the smooth operation of containerized applications. This section delves deeply into common issues encountered within Podman environments and outlines diagnostic strategies utilizing Podman's rich toolset.

Container performance can be hindered by various factors ranging from resource constraints, such as CPU and memory consumption, to misconfigurations in dependencies or environmental variables. Familiarity with the common problem profiles aids in efficient troubleshooting. This section explores the necessity of diagnosing these common container issues to maintain high operational efficiency and reliability.

Podman, a tool synonymous with simplicity and efficiency in managing pods and containers, provides a robust suite of diagnostic utilities. These utilities allow users to extract actionable insights into container behavior and pinpoint errors or misconfigurations with precision.

Identifying the root causes of issues often begins with basic monitoring and validation through logs, resource utilization assessments, and hardware or network diagnostics. When a container fails to start, underperforms, or exhibits erratic behavior, examining these areas methodically can unveil the underlying causes.

Podman's utilities feature a command-line interface (CLI) designed for proactive troubleshooting. Commands like `podman info`, `podman inspect`, and `podman logs` can significantly streamline the identification process for container issues. Here, we provide a detailed examination of these commands and illustrate their use with relevant examples to guide effective diagnostics.

To begin diagnosing issues with Podman containers, start by gathering comprehensive system information. The `podman info` command provides insights into the Podman version, running environment, storage, and networking settings. Executing this command can help verify the setup and identify discrepancies in configurations. For example:

```
podman info
```

This command output yields crucial information about the CPU architecture, kernel version, and the storage driver in use. It is important when diagnosing compatibility or performance issues that could stem from kernel or architecture-specific behaviors.

In situations where a specific container exhibits faults, `podman inspect` provides an in-depth view of the container's configuration and state. It returns low-level information about the configuration parameters passed during the container launch, environments, and filesystem details. This command is instrumental when validating expected configurations against the actual state. Consider the following example:

```
podman inspect <container-id>
```

The JSON output from the above command reveals detailed information about the container's Settings, HostConfig, and NetworkSettings, allowing the user to scrutinize aspects such as exposed ports, volumes, and network bindings. Analyzing differences between the expected and actual configurations can often lead to identifying misconfigurations that cause container applications to fail or misbehave.

271

Resource constraints represent a common source of container issues. Containers may experience throttling if they exceed granted CPU or memory limits. Using `podman stats`, users can monitor resource utilization in real-time across all containers:

```
podman stats
```

This command produces an interactive display of each container's CPU, memory, and network usage statistics. Identifying which containers are resource-saturated or are inefficiently utilizing resources may guide further tuning to improve performance. Adjusting container resource limits based on observed data can mitigate issues of resource contention.

Networking issues within containers can significantly impact application performance. Podman offers `podman network` commands to view and manage container network configurations. To troubleshoot network-related problems, ensure the correctness of network bindings and bridge configurations:

```
podman network ls
```

Listing available networks allows for the verification of network creation and associations. In conjunction with `podman inspect`, verifying the associated container networks can reveal mismatches or missing bridges that might obstruct connectivity.

In containers communicating with external systems, DNS and routing problems are prevalent. Checking the container's DNS configuration using `podman inspect` helps align the DNS resolutions with the host or configured resolvers. Misaligned DNS settings can lead to resolution failures, prompting further diagnostic testing with utilities like `ping` or `curl`.

Additionally, analyzing runtime logs from Podman and associated applications provides invaluable insights into the sequence of events leading to an issue. Accessing the logs is straightforward using `podman logs`:

```
podman logs <container-id>
```

The logs contain chronological records of system messages, error outputs, and application-specific logs coded by developers. Interpreting these logs can help identify errors such as missing environment variables, incorrect paths, or unhandled exceptions leading to container crashes.

Persistent issues may also stem from outdated or incompatible container images. Ensuring images are current and compatible with host environments helps prevent runtime errors. Removing unused or potentially corrupted images using:

```
podman rmi <image-id>
```

This helps maintain a clean, uncluttered system environment. Regular image updates and a defined image management policy facilitate smoother operations and reduced downtime due to outdated dependencies.

Podman also supports health checks to automatically diagnose and recover from faults. By specifying health checks within the container's definition, Podman can proactively resolve issues or report faults before they escalate:

```
podman run --health-cmd="curl -f http://localhost/ || exit 1" <image-
    id>
```

The parameter `--health-cmd` with a URL check example integrates a health checking mechanism to test web service availability within the container environment. Failed checks invoke pre-defined action plans, reducing manual intervention needs.

In summary, diagnosing common container issues in a Podman envi-

ronment involves a systematic approach leveraging Podman's extensive command suite. By examining runtime information, resource
utilization, network configurations, and application logs, developers
can effectively isolate, identify, and rectify issues. Efficient use of diagnostic tools not only sustains container stability but also enhances
the practitioner's understanding of containerized application environments, enabling informed optimizations and preemptive troubleshooting in future scenarios.

10.2.   Utilizing Logs for Troubleshooting

Logs are a vital component in the troubleshooting toolkit for containerized applications. They provide an immutable record of operations,
actions, and errors that occur within the system. In the context of
Podman containers, logs play a pivotal role in identifying issues and
tracking the execution flow of applications. This section examines the
extensive use of logs for troubleshooting purposes, detailing how to retrieve, interpret, and leverage log information to address a variety of
container-related problems.

A log is essentially a chronological collection of recorded data that captures events and states within a system. These include system-level
logs, application logs, and runtime logs that collectively provide comprehensive visibility into the operations within a containerized environment.

To troubleshoot effectively, the understanding and manipulation of
these logs must be mastered. Podman outputs distinct logs for different purposes. These logs are categorized as daemon logs, container
logs, and pod logs, offering varying granularity of information. This
section breaks down the process of utilizing each type of log for troubleshooting.

The starting point in log-based diagnostics is accessing the correct logs for the issue at hand. Podman utilizes `journald` for logging by default, but it can be configured to use alternative logging drivers such as JSON log files or local storage. Familiarity with the configured logging system is crucial. Logs stored by `journald` can be accessed using `journalctl` commands:

```
sudo journalctl -u podman
```

This command provides data from the Podman service log file, detailing service startup and operational messages. It aids in diagnosing broader issues related to container engine configuration and service-level failures, such as initialization errors or network conflicts.

Container-specific logs can be retrieved directly from the Podman CLI by using the `podman logs` command. This command conveys outputs from the container's `stdout` and `stderr` streams over its lifecycle:

```
podman logs <container-id>
```

Analyzing these logs involves looking for anomalies or messages indicating errors. Patterns such as repeated failures to access a file, connection errors, or stack traces point the administrator towards the component or configuration at fault.

For further diagnosis, consider employing filtering options to hone in on messages of interest. `Podman logs` supports tailing the latest logs, as well as retrieving logs between specific time frames. Such retrieval can be fine-tuned with:

```
podman logs --since="2023-10-01" --tail 100 <container-id>
```

The above command extracts logs generated since a specified date, displaying only the most recent entries. This is particularly useful in active environments with verbose logging output.

Content within logs is only as useful as the ability to extract actionable insights from it. This process involves decomposing log entries into meaningful sequences to uncover the root cause of a problem. Hence, understanding log structure and contents is crucial. Logs typically include timestamps, log levels, message source, and actual message data. Analyzing these elements can uncover patterns and provide clues about application state transitions and failures.

For example, examining log levels, such as ERROR, WARN, INFO, or DEBUG, helps prioritize focus on severe issues. A frequent ERROR level message may indicate a systemic problem requiring immediate attention. In contrast, DEBUG level entries might be leveraged during development and testing phases to enrich context around other log messages.

Extended log analysis often requires the integration of logs from multiple containers or services to map out interactions occurring between them. Consider using logging aggregation tools, such as the ELK (Elasticsearch, Logstash, and Kibana) stack, for collating and analyzing logs at scale. These tools provide robust search and visualization capabilities, making it feasible to correlate events across different parts of an application or infrastructure.

In addition to reactive troubleshooting, logs can support predictive diagnostics to prevent future issues. By monitoring logs over time, baseline behaviors and patterns can be established. Anomalies or deviations from these baselines may serve as early indicators of underlying issues, sparking preemptive actions. An appropriate logging strategy will thusly incorporate monitoring tools and alerting mechanisms to automate this process.

Alerts triggered by specific error instances or log volume spikes can be configured to elevate awareness of failing operations. System administrators may use these to set threshold-based alerts to notify when issues arise, facilitating a faster response.

Equally important is ensuring that logging does not itself become a source of issues. Logs should be managed carefully to prevent consumption of excessive storage or utilization that might degrade performance. Employ suitable log rotation and retention policies to maintain an optimal balance. In Podman, logs can be configured to rotate based on size and time parameters, ensuring stale logs are cleaned appropriately:

```
container:
  log_driver: journald
  log_opt:
    max-size: 10m
    max-file: 3
```

Within the Podman configuration files, adjust the `log_driver` and `log_opt` parameters in response to specific logging requirements, thus managing log growth and preserving critical space.

Podman allows for advanced logging configurations tailored to applications' needs. For scenario-specific logging, defining custom logging formats and adding contextual information within log messages can extend the effectiveness of troubleshooting and auditing practices. Contextual information might include application-specific parameters, environment details, request identifiers, and more, readily included and interpreted by modular logging systems.

Advanced users may opt for structured logging, conveying logs in formats like JSON, which facilitates analysis and consumption by parsing scripts and automation tools.

Logs are indispensable in diagnosing problems, fine-tuning performance, and enforcing reliability within containerized environments managed by Podman. By mastering the acquisition and analysis of log data, end-users gain the capacity to respond adeptly to operational challenges, thereby assuring the resilience and efficiency of their applications.

10.3. Optimizing Container Resource Usage

Efficient resource utilization is critical in managing containerized applications to maintain performance, maximize density, and reduce operational costs. Containers, by design, offer a lightweight and isolated environment, but without proper resource management, they can lead to resource contention, exhaustion, and, ultimately, system inefficiencies. This section explores methodologies to optimize resource usage within Podman-managed containers, focusing on CPU, memory, disk, and network resources.

Resource optimization within containers demands assessing the exact requirements of applications and the capabilities of the underlying infrastructure. The process involves fine-tuning the allocation of CPU and memory, managing disk space and I/O, and optimizing network bandwidth.

CPU Resource Management

The CPU represents the primary compute resource in any containerized environment. When multiple containers run concurrently on a host, they compete for CPU time, which can lead to performance degradation if not appropriately managed.

CPU Limits and Shares: Podman provides mechanisms to control the amount of CPU time allocated to containers through CPU shares, quotas, and periods. cpu-shares is a weight-based allocation that assigns greater CPU share to more critical containers relative to others:

```
podman run --cpu-shares=512 <image>
```

Here, 512 represents twice the default CPU share of 1024, granting the container proportionally more CPU time than one with the default allocation.

CPU Quotas: Further refined controls are possible using

278

--cpu-quota and --cpu-period, which directly limit CPU utilization. For instance, a 50% CPU limit can be set using:

```
podman run --cpu-quota=50000 --cpu-period=100000 <image>
```

cpu-quota restricts container use to the defined share of CPU time within each specified period cycle.

Careful calibration of these settings can significantly optimize CPU distribution, ensuring high-priority services receive adequate resources during peak loads while maintaining system responsiveness.

Memory Management

Memory is another critical resource for running applications inside containers. Insufficient memory allocation can cause applications to crash, while overallocation can lead to inefficient usage patterns.

Memory Limits: Specify memory limits with --memory to restrict the maximum amount of memory a container can use:

```
podman run --memory=512m <image>
```

Setting a limit enforces the container to auto-reclaim memory and limits its capacity to buffer large, unnecessary data sets.

Swap Space: The --memory-swap flag manages memory swap, useful for controlling the total of memory and swap the container can consume. Setting reasonable swap limits can help when memory limits approach their thresholds:

```
podman run --memory=512m --memory-swap=1g <image>
```

This allocation ensures that the combined memory and swap used do not exceed 1g, leveraging swap to avert out-of-memory (OOM) situations.

Memory Reservation: Use --memory-reservation to reserve a minimal amount of memory to ensure the container maintains a base level of memory resources, even during shared resource contention:

```
podman run --memory-reservation=256m <image>
```

Analyzing application memory profiles and configuring limits accordingly can diminish the occurrence of memory-related issues, enhancing container reliability and predictability.

Disk and I/O Optimization

Disk space and input/output (I/O) operations pose unique challenges in container environments. Optimizing disk use and I/O is vital to prevent bottlenecks and maintain performance.

Storage Drivers: Podman supports several storage backends like OverlayFS, Btrfs, and VFS, each having distinctive capabilities and trade-offs. OverlayFS is the default, suited for performance due to its layering support. Evaluating the file system interactions and selecting the ideal storage driver based on workload metrics is crucial.

Disk Quotas: Limit container filesystem size with `--storage-opt`, curtailing excessive disk usage:

```
podman run --storage-opt size=3G <image>
```

Controlling the maximum amount of storage ensures containers do not exhaust host disk space.

Volume Optimization: When using volumes, consider using `--read-only` mounts where write operations are unnecessary to improve performance and security:

```
podman run --read-only -v <vol>:/app/data:ro <image>
```

Monitoring disk I/O patterns and instituting limits inspire improved application runtime efficiencies. Setting up proper volume mounts and securing log rotations are integral part of optimized disk usage in a Podman environment.

Network Resource Optimization

Network performance impacts application throughput and latency. Hence, optimizing network resources is crucial for applications heavily reliant on data transfer.

Network Modes: The choice of network mode in Podman—bridge, host, none—impacts container accessibility and network performance:

```
podman run --network=bridge <image>
```

Bridge mode, the default, isolates container networks but adds a layer of NAT, affecting latency. Host mode confers direct host stack access, lowering latency but at some accessibility cost.

Traffic Control: Utilize network bandwidth controls to manage container traffic via tc (traffic control), shaping egress traffic and preventing congestion bottlenecks for time-sensitive applications.

DNS Configuration: Optimizing DNS settings for containerized applications ensures robust connectivity and service discovery:

```
podman run --dns=8.8.8.8 <image>
```

Precise DNS configurations and caching reduce latency in connection setup and safeguard connectivity across dynamic, multi-node deployments.

Network Security: Incorporate secure networking strategies (e.g., firewalls, IP whitelisting) to not only optimize performance but enhance overall security posture.

Holistic Optimization Approach

Profiling and Monitoring: Pre-emptive monitoring through tools like Prometheus and Grafana can predict workload demands and automatically adjust resource constraints, offering a proactive optimization framework.

281

Resource Scaling: Examine the use of orchestration platforms like Kubernetes, which provide automated scaling and resource optimization features for large-scale deployments. Properly configured horizontal pod autoscalers (HPA) align resources dynamically with workload demands.

Resource-Aware Scheduling: Implementation of intelligent resource scheduling, facilitated by precise resource requests and limitations, ensures balanced utilization across nodes and containers.

Best Practices: Regularly reviewing and updating container design patterns based on application profiling and evolving requirements supports ongoing performance improvements.

Optimization of container resource usage involves a continuous cycle of assessment and adjustment. By leveraging Podman's resource management capabilities effectively, a balance can be struck between resource constraints and application performance, thus yielding a highly optimized and efficient containerized environment. Such optimizations are crucial for sustaining operational excellence, reducing costs, and heightening the resiliency of applications within Podman-managed ecosystems.

10.4.   Improving Image Performance and Size

The performance and size of container images significantly impact the efficiency and scalability of containerized applications. Large images can slow down deployment processes, consume excessive network bandwidth, and require ample storage, affecting the overall performance of container orchestration. Furthermore, optimizing image performance and size enhances speed and reduces operational costs. This section provides a comprehensive exploration of strategies to streamline container image performance and reduce image size using tech-

282

niques applicable in Podman environments.

Container images encapsulate an application's code, runtime, libraries, and dependencies, offering self-contained execution environments irrespective of the host system. The encapsulation requirement means any optimization efforts must maintain functional integrity while reducing unnecessary bloat. A meticulous approach to image construction, layering, and management thus plays a pivotal role in performance enhancement.

Optimizing Image Layers

Image layers, the building blocks of container images, represent filesystem changes made during the image build process. Each 'Dockerfile' instruction creates a new layer, and hence optimizing these instructions is crucial.

Combining Instructions: To minimize layer count, consolidate multiple related instructions into a single command where feasible. This minimizes the number of layers and thus reduces the overall image size:

```
RUN apt-get update && apt-get install -y \
    package1 \
    package2
```

Here, combining 'apt-get update' and package installations minimizes the creation of intermediate layers.

Order of Instructions: Given each layer builds on the previous one, reordering 'RUN', 'COPY', and other instructions to prioritize frequently changed content later in the Dockerfile can further disk caching efficiency. Keeping stable base configuration higher up maximizes image cache reusability.

Layer Pruning: Actively remove files and reduce data retained post-installation within a single layer, thereby trimming down the resultant filesystem changes:

```
RUN apt-get update && apt-get install -y package3 && \
    apt-get clean && rm -rf /var/lib/apt/lists/*
```

The cleaning step herein ensures transient files are eliminated within
the same layer to save space.

Base Image Selection

Lightweight Base Images: Opt for minimal base images tailored
specifically for your application's requirements. Lightweight images,
such as those based on Alpine Linux, provide an entire functional
base with a nominal footprint, potentially reducing image sizes significantly:

```
FROM alpine:latest
```

Distroless Base Images: These images remove operating system
elements not necessary for running the application, providing an even
more reduced footprint and a heightened security posture by minimizing attack surface:

```
FROM gcr.io/distroless/base
```

Using lightweight or distroless base images demands ensuring all dependencies are explicitly defined, and associated binaries remain self-
sufficient without OS utilities.

Dependency Management

Optimized Package Management: Analyze and question the necessity of each package installed within the image. This scrutiny ensures only the minimum working set of dependencies reside in the final
build:

```
RUN npm install --production
```

Opting for production-only dependency installations in Node.js applications, for instance, avoids undesired size growth.

Static Binaries: For applications primarily compiled into binaries, evaluate compiling with static linking to encapsulate necessary libraries within the binary itself, reducing external library dependencies.

Efficient Resource Packaging

Multi-Stage Builds: A revolutionary method in Dockerfiles, employed to create artifacts in one stage that doesn't carry over to the final image, significantly trims image size by excluding build dependencies:

```
FROM golang AS builder
WORKDIR /app
COPY . .
RUN go build -o myapp

FROM alpine:latest
COPY --from=builder /app/myapp /usr/bin/myapp
```

Lean Environmental Setup: Remove development tools, documentation files, and any superfluous data employed during the build process from the final image. Utilize targeted COPY commands for copying only the required files.

Security and Compliance Checks

Regular Updates: Continuously update base images and dependencies to their latest stable versions. Using automated build pipelines integrated with vulnerability scanners, such as Clair or Trivy, identifies and mitigates security risks associated with container images.

Signature Verification: Prioritize images from trusted registry sources and validate image signatures to ascertain authenticity and integrity.

Performance Considerations

Cincinnati Redundancy: Leverage Podman's layered caching to avoid rebuilds unless source files change. Craft Dockerfiles that respect this principle, ensuring frequent revisions do not invalidate cached assets.

Effective Caching: Podman's build and run cache mechanisms, manipulated through caching configurations and precise layering, encourage efficiency. 'podman build"s '–no-cache' flag or refining 'COPY .' commands can tighten control over this behavior.

In addition to these methods, incorporating continuous integration and deployment practices ensures recent, optimized images are always available. Image scanning tools paired with automated rebuild pipelines permit swift adoption of base image updates, enhancing both performance and security.

An overarching perspective considers compliance with organizational standards balancing lean image construction and operational requirements. Formulating standardized, versioned, and clean image architecture mitigates size bloat while maximizing performance incorporations within Podman-managed environments. These practices, collectively adopted, translate into faster deployments, more agile operations, reduced costs, and an elevated security posture for containerized applications.

10.5. Enhancing Networking Performance

Networking is a critical component of containerized infrastructure, serving as the backbone for communication between containers, services, and external networks. In container orchestration environments such as those managed by Podman, optimizing networking performance is crucial to ensure low latency, high bandwidth, and robust connectivity. This section focuses on enhancing networking performance for containers, exploring methods to optimize configuration, manage resources, and enhance security.

A thorough understanding of networking models and configurations specific to Podman is essential for optimizing container networks. Podman allows for various networking setups that include 'bridge', 'host', and 'slirp4netns' modes, each catering to different performance and security needs. Mastering these configurations allows administrators to tailor network behavior to application requirements while maximizing performance.

Podman supports several networking modes which influence container connectivity and performance attributes. The correct mode selection impacts throughput, latency, and isolation levels within containerized systems.

Bridge Mode: This default mode creates a virtualized network bridge wherein containers batch traffic with Network Address Translation (NAT) allowing outbound connectivity. Opt for bridge mode when isolating networks between containers is necessary:

```
podman run --network=bridge <image>
```

Bridge networks can be configured with custom subnets, IP address ranges, and DNS settings, offering control over container IP allocation and communication paths. This mode maintains host isolation while enabling access to container networks via forwarded ports.

Host Mode: Utilizing host mode removes virtualized network layers, enabling containers to share the host's network stack. This mode offers minimal latency and overhead, beneficial for performance-demanding applications, but forsakes container network isolation:

```
podman run --network=host <image>
```

Leveraging host mode is ideal for services requiring rapid data flow or high processing rates, where security implications from network expo-

287

sure are managed by other safeguards.

Slirp4netns Mode: When rootless deployments are in place, employ slirp4netns mode to proxy container traffic through the host network stack without requiring root privileges:

```
podman run --network=slirp4netns <image>
```

Each mode bears performance trade-offs related to security and operational requirements. Evaluate the appropriate setup based on the container's role and required isolation.

Network configurations must be optimized for high throughput and low latency to foster seamless interaction between components in distributed systems.

Quality of Service (QoS): By implementing QoS policies, applications can prioritize specific traffic categories, mitigating the effects of concurrent network-intensive tasks. Use traffic shaping with utilities like 'tc' to control packet queuing, enhance packet transmission, or throttle non-critical network flows.

DNS Resolution: Fine-tuning DNS configurations can substantially improve latency. Running a local DNS cache or employing DNS servers with minimal response times reduces latency during DNS lookups:

```
podman run --dns=<dns-server> <image>
```

Offloading Capabilities: Utilize hardware network interface controllers (NICs) with offloading capabilities to reduce processor load by transferring network layer operations to the NIC. While configuring network hardware, enable TCP segmentation offload (TSO) or large receive offload (LRO) to benefit applications processing substantial network traffic.

Dynamic resource allocation ensures container networks adapt to workload demands, preserving performance across varying conditions.

Bandwidth Limitations: Defining bandwidth and data rate restrictions optimizes traffic flow, preventing any single container from monopolizing network resources:

```
tc qdisc add dev <device> root tbf rate 1gbit burst 32kbit latency
    400ms
```

Implement policies for shaping outbound traffic that adhere to the topology of network interfaces, accommodating both throughput constraints and application requirements.

Multithreading and Concurrency: Maximize the number of concurrent processing threads for applications under substantial load. Ensure applications exploit parallelism efficiently and application architectures are conducive to API endpoints and services scaling linearly with growing traffic.

Enhancing network performance cannot come at the expense of security. Integrated measures to secure container networks should accompany optimization, supporting a comprehensive approach.

Network Policies: Implement network policies regulating traffic permissions based on predefined rules, enforcing strict connectivity control between containers and external services.

Encryption: Use encryptions, such as TLS for intra-service communications, establishing secure channels that prevent data interception or tampering:

```
podman run --network=bridge -v <path-to-cert>:/etc/ssl/certs/<cert> <
    image>
```

This added layer of security ensures data integrity and confidentiality, essential to safeguarding sensitive operations when enhancing performance.

289

Network Segmentation: Strategically segment networks to isolate sensitive or critical workloads, reducing attack exposure, ensuring security while meeting performance benchmarks. Design VLANs or overlay networks within Podman's capabilities, guided by application requirements.

To sustain optimized network performance, frequent monitoring and maintenance are imperative.

Network Monitoring Tools: Leverage tools like Prometheus, Grafana, and Wireshark to collect metrics and observe traffic patterns at both macro and micro scales, providing real-time insight into network status and bottlenecks.

Automated Alerts: Implement automated alert systems built upon monitoring data to notify administrators of anomalies or threshold breaches that may degrade performance. Timely alerts enable quick interventions and proactive adjustments.

Performance Testing: Regularly conduct load testing and stress simulations using tools such as Apache JMeter or Kubernetes' K8s-bench to validate network performance under various simulated conditions, ensuring it meets the expectations set by business and application needs.

Enhancing networking performance within Podman-managed container environments involves a balance of thoughtful configuration, security, and continuous oversight. Implementing network policies, resource optimization strategies, and advanced monitoring practices will foster efficient, reliable, and secure networks. This focused approach plays a crucial role in maintaining the agility and robustness of containerized infrastructure, ultimately elevating organizational capability to meet demanding digital expectations.

10.6. Monitoring and Tuning Podman for Performance

Maintaining optimal performance in containerized environments is critical for ensuring that applications run efficiently and meet service-level agreements. In pod-based container management systems like Podman, comprehensive monitoring and proactive tuning play pivotal roles in sustaining and improving performance over time. This section delves into methodologies and tools for monitoring Podman containers and provides insights into tuning practices to optimize performance continually.

Monitoring encompasses collecting, processing, and analyzing metrics to acquire visibility into container operations. These metrics highlight various aspects such as CPU load, memory usage, network latency, and I/O operations. Efficient monitoring facilitates timely detection of bottlenecks and aids decision-making for resource allocation and optimization. Podman's close integration with systemd and the Linux ecosystem provides a viable framework for integrated monitoring solutions.

Monitoring Tools and Techniques

Podman Native Monitoring: Podman offers built-in commands like podman stats that provide real-time information about running containers. It reports metrics like CPU, memory, and network usage, allowing for quick assessments:

```
podman stats --all
```

This command gives a snapshot view of resource utilization across all running containers, highlighting potential bottlenecks at a glance.

System-Level Monitoring with Systemd: Podman containers are typically managed as systemd services, making systemd journal logs a

291

rich resource for monitoring. Using `journalctl`, administrators can
retrieve logs and service-related events:

```
sudo journalctl -u podman
```

Third-Party Monitoring Solutions: Integrating robust monitoring solutions such as Prometheus for metrics collection and Grafana
for visualization can expand the scope and granularity of monitoring:

```
- job_name: 'podman'
  static_configs:
    - targets: ['localhost:8080']
```

This configuration snippet for Prometheus adds a job to scrape metrics
exposed by containers, enabling detailed analysis and historical tracking of container-specific metrics.

Performance Metrics and Interpretation

Effective performance tuning requires understanding the significance
of key metrics and their implication on containerized environments.

CPU Utilization: Tracking CPU usage for containers identifies overcommitment and competition for processing time. High sustained utilization may indicate the need for resource reallocation or increased
system capacity.

- Metric Evaluation: CPU usage close to 100% over long periods
  suggests saturation.

- Tuning Strategy: Adjust container CPU quotas or increase the
  number of CPU cores available to the host.

Memory Usage: Memory metrics highlight consumption patterns
and potential spikes leading to OOM situations. Consistently high
memory usage can degrade performance by causing swap usage.

- Metric Evaluation: Monitor memory and swap usage through

low-level system metrics.

- Tuning Strategy: Set memory limits to prevent overuse, employ memory reservations to guarantee availability, and optimize application code for memory efficiency.

Network Traffic: Examine network metrics for throughput and latency indications. Traffic bottlenecks often appear in high-latency or saturated bandwidth scenarios.

- Metric Evaluation: High latency and low throughput suggest network inefficiency.

- Tuning Strategy: Optimize network configurations, implement load balancing, and review network modes or policies.

I/O Performance: Disk I/O metrics inform on read/write speeds and reveal hotspots where contention is delaying operations.

- Metric Evaluation: Look for high I/O wait times or saturated throughput.

- Tuning Strategy: Balance storage backends, consider fast SSDs for high I/O applications, and use performance-tuned filesystems like XFS or Btrfs.

Tuning Practices for Podman Performance Enhancement

Tuning strategies vary based on specific workloads and operational demands. Emphasizing a performance-centric configuration ensures optimizations are both effective and sustainable.

Resource Limits and Shares: Setting appropriate resource boundaries ensures fair allocation among containers. Utilize Podman's limits for CPU and memory to control resource utilization effectively.

Process Isolation and Optimization: Use cgroups and namespaces for enforcing strict process isolation, minimizing interference between various container processes:

```
podman run --cgroup-parent=/my/cgroup <image>
```

Seccomp and AppArmor Profiles: Tailor security profiles to balance performance with security, disabling unnecessary features that consume resources. Custom profiles reduce latency induced by security checks.

Storage Optimization: Employ multi-stage builds, lean base images, and layer optimization practices to create efficient and performance-oriented container images, lightweight to facilitate rapid loading and execution:

```
FROM alpine AS builder
...
FROM scratch
COPY --from=builder /path/to/binary /binary
```

Automated Tuning and CI/CD Integration

Embed tuning practices into continuous integration and deployment pipelines, ensuring they adaptively apply in response to monitored metrics:

- **Trigger Autoscaling**: Use feedback loops from monitoring systems to trigger automated scaling policies that dynamically adjust container counts and resource allocations based on performance demands.

- **Policy-Based Management**: Implement policies that automatically apply configuration changes under specific conditions, utilizing scripting and orchestration tools to enforce adaptable changes promptly.

- **Regular Audits**: Perform routine assessments and audits of

294

current configurations against performance data trends to identify under-utilization or over-subscription.

Monitoring and tuning Podman containers involves a multiphase approach focusing on ongoing visibility and responsiveness to performance data. Deploying a systemic, metrics-driven methodology supports a cosmos where container operations align with application
needs, reducing latency, maximizing efficiency, and optimizing resource utilization across diverse environments. Integrated with strategic scheduling, targeted resource allocations, and continuous monitoring, Podman can deliver a robust performance-oriented container
management solution. Through these practices, operations teams can
sustain high availability, ensure compliance with service expectations,
and retain control over sprawling workloads in dynamic ecosystems.